THE MYSTERY OF THE RED HEIFER

MONDO GONZALES

THE MYSTERY OF THE RED HEIFER by Mondo Gonzales
Published by Charisma House, an imprint of Charisma Media
1150 Greenwood Blvd., Lake Mary, Florida 32746

Copyright © 2025 by Mondo Gonzales. All rights reserved.

Unless otherwise noted, all Scripture quotations are taken are from The ESV® Bible (The Holy Bible, English Standard Version®), copyright © 2001 by Crossway, a publishing ministry of Good News Publishers. Used by permission. All rights reserved.

Scripture quotations marked KJV are from the King James Version of the Bible.

Scripture quotations marked NASB are taken from the (NASB®) New American Standard Bible®, Copyright © 1960, 1971, 1977, 1995 by The Lockman Foundation. Used by permission. All rights reserved. www.lockman.org

Scripture quotations marked NET are from the NET Bible® copyright ©1996-2016 by Biblical Studies Press, L.L.C. http://netbible.com. All rights reserved.

Scripture quotations marked NIV are taken from the Holy Bible, New International Version®, NIV®. Copyright © 1973, 1978, 1984, 2011 by Biblica, Inc.® Used by permission of Zondervan. All rights reserved worldwide. www.zondervan.com. The "NIV" and "New International Version" are trademarks registered in the United States Patent and Trademark Office by Biblica, Inc.®

Scripture quotations marked NKJV are taken from the New King James Version®. Copyright © 1982 by Thomas Nelson. Used by permission. All rights reserved.

While the author has made every effort to provide accurate, up-to-date source information at the time of publication, statistics and other data are constantly updated. Neither the publisher nor the author assumes any responsibility for errors or for changes that occur after publication. Further, the publisher and author do not have any control over and do not assume any responsibility for third-party websites or their content.

Mondo Gonzales is a first-class researcher! He leaves no stone or ancient text unturned. His pursuit of the truth is unfaltering while his ability to read the ancient texts in their original language only adds to his efforts to uncover biblical truths.

The Mystery of the Red Heifer is a timely tome that delves into the ancient prophetic texts that make the Bible the most unique and stand-alone book on the planet. Mondo has done an in-depth study of the ancient ritual of the red heifer in all its complexities and how it dovetails with the prophecies that are yet to be fulfilled—perhaps in our lifetimes.

This book will take you on a journey into Israel's ancient past and then into modernity as we see how important this rite of purification is to the rebuilding of the third temple. I look forward to seeing where Mondo will take us if the Lord tarries, as he has a lot of intellectual irons in the fire!

—L. A. MARZULLI
AUTHOR, LECTURER, FILMMAKER

The Holy Bible is the book of prophecy that clearly reveals future events. One of these events is the building of the third temple in Jerusalem. But before the temple is complete, the fulfillment of the prophecy of the red heifer must take place.

In his eye-opening new book, *The Mystery of the Red Heifer*, Mondo Gonzales reveals that prophecy is being fulfilled and the red heifers that could herald the rebuilding of the temple on Mount Moriah possibly exist. All of this indicates that the return of Jesus is imminent.

—LARRY OLLISON, PHD, THD
AUTHOR, PASTOR, DEAN, INTERNATIONAL SPEAKER

I heartily recommend this book for all students of Bible prophecy, whether advanced or just starting their journey. Mondo covers the subject of the red heifer from every vital angle—biblical, doctrinal, historical, rabbinical, prophetic—with the wealth of understanding you would expect from a scholar, yet delivered in a down-to-earth presentation that remains accessible to the average reader. What is the significance of the red heifers? Are they necessary for the temple service? Do they come before or after the temple? What are the necessary qualifications for a red heifer? What is the relationship between the biblical and the rabbinical handling of the red heifer? All these questions and more will be answered.

—LEE BRAINARD
PROPHECY TEACHER, SOOTHKEEP.INFO

At a time when fanciful speculation and unfettered spiritualizing are rampant within the Bible prophecy movement, Mondo Gonzales has provided a solid, reliable treatment of a widely misunderstood topic: the red heifers. With a rare combination of scholarship and readability, and emanating from a consistent dispensational framework, *The Mystery of the Red Heifer* takes the reader from the biblical text, through Jewish history, and into the modern discussion in a way that removes the mystery and leaves the reader saying, "Oh, I see now. That makes perfect sense!" This book is tailor-made for anyone who desires to learn the important implications of the red heifer movement without the unnecessary hype.

—J. B. HIXSON, PHD
NOTBYWORKS.ORG

How can we know that Jesus Christ is coming back soon? Look to Israel, the super sign! Mondo yet again spellbinds students of Bible prophecy, helping us gain clarity and insight into one of the greatest mysteries concerning Israel's long journey back to their Messiah. You'll find few people more enthusiastic about the return of the red heifers than Mondo, and after reading his fascinating research, you too will share in his excitement for our great King's glorious return to the earth.

—NATHAN E. JONES, PHD
INTERNET EVANGELIST, LAMB & LION MINISTRIES
CHRISTINPROPHECY.ORG

For more resources like this, visit MyCharismaShop.com and the author's website at prophecywatchers.com.

Cataloging-in-Publication Data is on file with the Library of Congress.
International Standard Book Number: 978-1-63641-473-7
E-book ISBN: 978-1-63641-474-4

$PrintCode
Printed in the United States of America

Most Charisma Media products are available at special quantity discounts for bulk purchase for sales promotions, premiums, fundraising, and educational needs. For details, call us at (407) 333-0600 or visit our website at charismamedia.com.

Contents

1. The Mystery of the Red Heifer 1
2. Why Should We Care About Some Red Cows? 5
3. Handling Objections to the Existence of a Physical Third Temple 21
4. The Red Heifer in the Bible 26
5. The Red Heifer in Rabbinic Tradition 36
6. Rabbis' Changing Views in Recent Years 59
7. The Pre-Temple Preparations 69
8. The Modern Search for the Red Heifer 77
9. The New Testament Significance of the Red Heifer ... 88
10. Your Favorite Prophecy Teachers Respond to the Red Heifer Movement 97
11. Seeking a Balanced Biblical Outlook on the Red Heifer Movement 128
12. Some Common Questions 151
13. Concluding Thoughts on the Red Heifer Movement ... 158

Appendix A   Second Thessalonians 2:3—A Jewish Apostasy or Church Apostasy? 160

Appendix B   Alfred Edersheim on the Temple's Ministry and Services at the Time of Christ 185

Appendix C   Josephus Discusses the Red Heifer 189

Notes 190

About the Author 199

Chapter 1

THE MYSTERY OF THE RED HEIFER

WE ARE LIVING in exciting times! Regardless of our religious background, almost everyone understands that the world today is different than it was even a few years ago. The global situation is changing at a rapid pace, and we are heading toward the final conflict at the end of the age, also known as the seven-year tribulation period. Jesus described this time as the worst in the history of creation (Mark 13:19).

We will go into detail about how the current global situation connects with prophetic signs of the coming Jewish third temple in the following chapters. Yet one of the most mysterious and intriguing elements in all of eschatology (the study of the last days) is the reinstatement of the red heifer ceremony and its role in the rebuilding of the temple and the fulfillment of end-time prophecy.

Jewish rabbis for millennia have expressed their wonder and awe at the commandment in Numbers 19 requiring the ashes of a red heifer for purification. In fact, they have deemed it one of the most mysterious prescriptions in the entire Bible. Rabbi Chaim Richman, an authority on the temple who is involved with the Temple Institute, an organization in Israel focused on building a third temple, wrote a book back in the 1990s called *The Mystery of the Red Heifer* in which he discusses the various ways rabbis struggled to understand the enigma of the red heifer ritual and why its ashes are needed before a third temple can be built. In order to understand the mystery, we must first address the concept of ritual impurity.

CLEAN OR UNCLEAN VS. FORGIVEN OR UNFORGIVEN

As New Covenant (New Testament) believers, we do not often think in terms of being ceremonially clean or unclean (pure or impure). We are more inclined to focus on the concept of being forgiven or unforgiven. This perspective is accurate because we are a spiritual people and are not required to go to a physical temple at least three times a year to make sacrifices as was done under the old covenant.

> Three times a year all your males shall appear before the LORD your God at the place that he will choose: at the Feast of Unleavened Bread, at the Feast of Weeks, and at the Feast of Booths. They shall not appear before the LORD empty-handed.
> —DEUTERONOMY 16:16

By faith in Christ we are purified and eternally forgiven through the once-and-for-all sacrifice of Jesus (Heb. 9:13–14; 10:1–14). Jesus also predicted there would be a time after His departure when a physical temple (and sacrifices) would not be necessary to worship and approach the Father in spirit and in truth (John 4:21–25).

However, since modern religious Jews have not yet accepted Jesus' sacrifice for their sins, they think only in terms of the Old Testament Mosaic system and its emphasis on sacrifices within a temple context. For them, this system does include forgiveness for sins but involves the standard of being clean or unclean in a ritual sense. God gave very specific instructions for approaching Him in the tabernacle or temple precincts.

Because the temple will be rebuilt on the Temple Mount, the area must be ritually cleansed before construction begins. In order to accomplish this cleansing, many believe the ashes are needed from a burned (slaughtered) red heifer, which will be mixed with water as outlined in Numbers 19. We will discuss these details in full in a subsequent chapter, but for now let me introduce one of the cryptic aspects of the commandment God gave in Numbers 19. Moses wrote:

> And a *man who is clean shall gather up the ashes* of the heifer and deposit them outside the camp in a *clean* place. And they shall be kept for the water for impurity for the congregation of the people of Israel; it is a sin offering. And *the one who gathers the ashes* of the heifer shall wash his clothes and *be unclean* until evening. And this shall be a perpetual statute for the people of Israel, and for the stranger who sojourns among them.
> —NUMBERS 19:9–10, EMPHASIS ADDED

Commenting on this passage, Barry Holtz, PhD, a professor of Jewish education at The Jewish Theological Seminary, wrote, "Adding to the mystery is the fact that those who are impure become purified, but those who are *already* pure and then come in contact with the ashes of the heifer become *impure* (Num. 19:10)."[1] These commandments were considered puzzling, causing much consternation through the ages as the various rabbinic sages sought to understand them.

Maimonides, a twelfth-century Spanish rabbi and philosopher also known as "Rambam," wrote prolifically and penned an applicable work called *The Guide for the Perplexed*. In his guide Maimonides discussed how some of God's commandments are inexplicable.

> Our Sages...hold that even these [mysterious] ordinances have a cause, and are certainly intended for some use, although it is not known to us; owing either to the deficiency of our knowledge or the weakness of our intellect.... You certainly know the famous saying that Solomon knew the reason for all commandments except that of the "red heifer." Our Sages also said that God concealed the causes of [some] commandments, lest people should despise them, as Solomon did in respect to three commandments, the reason for which is clearly stated. In this sense they always speak; and Scriptural texts support the idea.[2]

As Christians, we understand that Solomon was the wisest king who ever lived (1 Kings 3:12). As wise as he was, Jewish sages proclaim that even Solomon was not wise enough to understand the mystery of the red heifer commandment.

It is not surprising, then, that rabbis through the last two thousand years have not fully understood the mystery of the red heifer. Jesus said He came to fulfill the Law in all its aspects (Matt. 5:17), and we know all His actions fulfilled the will of the Father and that He lived a perfect life of obedience to all of God's commandments (Matt. 3:15; John 6:38).

Paul wrote that when the Jews read the Old Testament, they do so in a state of blindness and ignorance, yet if they were to receive Jesus as Messiah, the blinders (or veil) would be lifted, and they would understand that Jesus is the fulfillment of all aspects of the Law (2 Cor. 3:14-16). This includes the red heifer and is discussed in the Book of Hebrews. We will cover this in chapter 9 on the New Testament significance of the red heifer.

In the next chapter we will begin exploring what makes the red heifer such an important issue. In fact, many rabbis say the entire fate of the world depends on the red heifer ceremony. In a very narrow sense, they are correct. We know Bible prophecy must be fulfilled, and this includes the building of a third temple, which must be preceded by the slaughter of a red heifer.

Chapter 2

WHY SHOULD WE CARE ABOUT SOME RED COWS?

EVER SINCE ISRAEL became a nation in 1948, prophecy watchers have been eagerly awaiting the day when the Lord will return to call His bride home. Among the present convergence of dozens of prophetic signs, on September 15, 2022, five red heifers were shipped from Texas and landed in Israel. By reading this book, you will gain an understanding of the prophetic significance of this arrival and receive enough background information to recognize the importance of the red heifer movement.

Although the story of the red heifer begins with Moses around 1400 BC, it is active in our current time! The first thing to address is, "What is a heifer?" Simply put, a heifer is a two- or three-year-old female cow. It is not a calf nor is it a bull (male cow). For many Christians the excitement about these five heifers in Israel and around the world has become quite intense. The Temple Institute maintains a cautious optimism that at least one of these five red heifers will remain qualified and be ritually slaughtered in the near future.

There is also the risk that some Christians will misunderstand exactly what I mean by saying, "We are living in exciting times." The Bible has dozens, if not hundreds, of prophetic passages that help us understand the events leading up to the second coming of Jesus. Many of these prophecies contain serious information and reveal terrible judgments coming upon the earth during the seven-year tribulation period, when billions will perish. Jesus said this period will be unlike anything that has ever occurred in the history of the creation (Mark 13:19). The Bible also reveals that the Jewish people will be deceived by the Antichrist and undergo severe persecution during this time.

Am I excited for death and judgment? Not at all! When prophecy watchers get excited, it is because we see signs being fulfilled that point to the imminent return of Jesus, when He will begin to make all things right. We are excited about His return. It does not mean that we condone or approve of the new world order, the cashless system, or even the slaughter of the red heifer. I intend for this book to help the Bible-believing Christian understand the prophetic significance of the red heifer movement and the preparations that have been made to build the third temple.

In order to gain this understanding, it benefits us to review a brief outline of the prophetic importance and timeline of Israel becoming a nation in 1948 and how the Temple Mount continues to be a place of tension between the Jewish people and their neighbors.

The Founding and Religious Climate of Modern Israel

David Ben-Gurion, the first prime minister of Israel, made a worldwide declaration announcing the independent State of Israel on May 14, 1948. The situation in 1948 was tense, and Israel's Arab neighbors immediately attacked them the following day (May 15, 1948). After a drawn-out series of conflicts, Israel signed armistice agreements with all the attackers by July 1949. Israel had become an official nation, and it became a member of the United Nations on May 11, 1949.

Several more skirmishes followed in the coming decade, but the next conflict with prophetic implications is known as the Six-Day War, which took place June 5–10, 1967. For the first time since AD 70, the Jewish people gained control of Jerusalem and the Old City, including the Temple Mount!

Many people do not know that Israel was founded by those who generally considered themselves socialists. Even though it was founded as a parliamentary democracy, it was not overly influenced by the religious demographic. In order to understand the current prophetic atmosphere surrounding Israel and the Temple Mount, one must recognize how different the State of Israel is now than it was at its founding more than seventy-five years ago. The typical Jewish religious rabbinic opinion in the mid-twentieth century was that modern Israel was founded by secularists and therefore had no real religious legitimacy in their eyes. They held the belief that God Himself would miraculously create a Jewish state if that were His will.

So, let's venture back to 1967 when Israel conquered its enemies once again and regained control of Jerusalem—and more specifically, the Temple Mount area. The Jewish people had been forbidden to pray at the Western Wall (also called the *Kotel*) and on the Temple Mount after the 1949 Armistice Agreement and had no access to western Jerusalem from 1948 to 1967. After the 1967 Six-Day War and nineteen years of Jordanian rule, the Western Wall came under Israeli control and more than 200,000 Jews flocked to the Western Wall. This was seen as the first mass Jewish pilgrimage to the Western Wall since AD 70.

However, this nationalistic fervor would not last, as Defense Minister Moshe Dayan, a self-proclaimed atheist, made an agreement on June 17, 1967, with the Muslim religious authority over the Temple Mount, known as the Jerusalem Waqf. Jews would be allowed to visit inside the Temple Mount (but could not pray) and have access to the Western Wall, but full religious authority over the Temple Mount would remain with the Islamic Waqf, while political and security sovereignty remained with the State of Israel.[1]

A variety of diverse religious opinions existed at the time related to this decision. It would be helpful to note that the chief rabbis had issued a declaration forbidding any Jew to enter the Temple Mount area. They saw Defense Minister Dayan's political decision as helpful to enforce their declaration forbidding all Jews (especially religious Jews) from going up on the Temple Mount. A few Orthodox religious groups have consistently ignored these prohibitions, but the consensus of rabbis has always been that Jews are forbidden to go up on the Temple Mount.

The status quo of the Temple Mount has changed very little since 1967. However, during the last fifteen years—and especially since November 1, 2022, with the latest election of Benjamin Netanyahu and the most religious government in the history of modern Israel—there have been tremendous ramifications for the status of the Temple Mount, the coming third temple, and of course, the red heifer.

Why Should We Care About the Red Heifer?

We now return to the original question of this chapter: Why should we even care about the red heifer movement? Does it matter? What is the importance of all these efforts? When it comes to understanding eschatology, the study of last things, a diversity of beliefs exist among genuine Christians today. It is not my goal here to survey all the various beliefs but to point out that some believers see no significance to Israel becoming a nation or even its gaining control over Jerusalem. Others view it as interesting and possibly significant, but not important enough to address in a Sunday morning sermon.

On the other hand, I have known believers who only read texts on eschatology and don't have a good grasp on other areas of theology. As in anything, we should maintain a proper balance. The most important topic that a follower of Jesus should be well-versed in is sharing and articulating the good news about Jesus—that He is the only way for people to be reconciled to God the Father. (See Acts 4:12; John 14:6; and Romans 3:23; 6:23; 5:8; and 10:9.) At the same time, however, Jesus instructed us to watch for the signs and be ready for Him to return at any moment.

Jesus scolded the Pharisees of His day for not understanding Messianic prophecy related to His first coming.

> And the Pharisees and Sadducees came, and to test him they asked him to show them a sign from heaven. He answered them, "When it is evening, you say, 'It will be fair weather, for the sky is red.' And in the morning, 'It will be stormy today, for the sky is red and threatening.' You know how to interpret the appearance of the sky, but you cannot interpret the signs of the times. An evil and adulterous generation seeks for a sign, but no sign will be given to it except the sign of Jonah." So he left them and departed.
> —Matthew 16:1-4

When it comes to Messianic prophecy related to His second coming, Jesus gave extensive descriptions of what the end of the age would be like in various sermons (Luke 17:22-37), including what is known as the Olivet Discourse (Matt. 24:1-26:2; Mark 13:1-37; Luke 21:5-36). After giving precise details, He commanded all of His followers:

> Therefore stay awake—for you do not know when the master of the house will come, in the evening, or at midnight, or when the rooster crows, or in the morning—lest he come suddenly and find you asleep. And what I say to you I say to all: Stay awake.
> —Mark 13:35-37

To put it another way, we must be watching. As followers of Jesus, we do not have the luxury of dismissing Jesus' words or else we would fall into the same category as the first-century Pharisees. We are not required to become experts in eschatology, but we are required to have enough understanding to know what to watch for as Jesus said we should.

Watching for the Third Temple

One prophetic marker to watch for is the announcement of preparations to build, or the actual building of, the third temple in Jerusalem on the Temple Mount. I will cover the details of those preparations in a subsequent chapter, but for now I think it would be helpful to share why we believe a third temple will be built and how it connects to the red heifer.

The Bible does not always give us the absolute, complete picture or details of how prophecy is to be fulfilled. For example, consider the prophecy that the Messiah would be born in Bethlehem of Judea:

> But you, O Bethlehem Ephrathah, who are too little to be among the clans of Judah, from you shall come forth for me one who is to be ruler in Israel, whose coming forth is from of old, from ancient days.
> —Micah 5:2

The only clue this prophecy offers is that the Messiah would come from Bethlehem. It does not reveal how or when. As we come to the Gospels, we learn how God moved a pagan Roman emperor (Prov. 21:1) to issue a census that caused Joseph and Mary to travel eighty miles from Nazareth to their ancestral home in order to be registered. During that time, Jesus was born in Bethlehem, as we learn in Matthew 2. Thus, the prophecy of Micah 5:2 was fulfilled in an unexpected way.

Prophecy is most often a "snapshot" of the circumstances in a particular time and place. The prophet is given a word, a dream, or a vision of this time period. When it comes to understanding why prophecy watchers expect a third temple, we interpret a snapshot into the future from several prophets. Each prophet gives us insight concerning the final day of the Lord, which is also called the tribulation period or the seventieth week of Daniel.

WHY BELIEVE THERE WILL BE A PHYSICAL THIRD TEMPLE?

Let's begin in the Old Testament with the prophet Daniel. We do not have space to cover the entire seventy weeks of Daniel, but the last verse of chapter 9 concerns us the most, as it describes the events of the last week that are yet to be fulfilled. Daniel writes:

> And he shall make a strong covenant with many for one week, and for half of the week he shall *put an end to sacrifice and offering*. And on the wing of abominations shall come one who makes desolate, until the decreed end is poured out on the desolator.
>
> —DANIEL 9:27, EMPHASIS ADDED

From this passage we learn that at the "half" point of the week (the three-and-a-half-year mark out of the seven years) the Antichrist will put an end to sacrifices and offerings. Which sacrifices? Which offerings? The temple was destroyed in AD 70, and there have not been sacrifices made in Jerusalem on the Temple Mount for more than 1,900 years.

Let's go back to the concept that Daniel had received a snapshot of a future time period. In this future end-time scenario he saw sacrifices and offerings taking place. This seems confusing because there is no temple today for those sacrifices and offerings to take place. So, what should we conclude?

First, some people take the position that Daniel was speaking figuratively or symbolically. However, the symbolic interpretation of Daniel 9:27 does not make much sense because once you begin to spiritualize interpretations, you cannot land at a solid conclusion, and the interpretation becomes completely subjective to the reader.

Secondly, we could say that this prophecy was already fulfilled, as other Bible teachers claim. This does not make much sense either because the purposes of the seventy weeks prophecy found in Daniel 9:24-27 were clearly not fulfilled.

The third alternative is that even though we do not see a temple today, in order for this prophecy to be fulfilled, a temple *must* be built sometime in the future. The third temple will at least be built and in operation for sacrifices by the midpoint of the tribulation period. It could be finished one day before the midpoint, or years prior. The interpretation that a temple will be rebuilt in the future is based on a logical deduction from the text itself and grounded in the conviction that when God gives a prophecy, it absolutely must come to pass, or else God would be a liar.

Even though we might not understand how a prophecy could come to pass nor believe it to be possible, God cannot fail. Notice what God says about prophecy in Isaiah 46:9-11 (emphasis added):

> Remember the former things of old; for I am God, and there is no other; I am God, and there is none like me, declaring the end from the beginning and from ancient times things not yet done, saying, "*My counsel shall stand, and I will accomplish all my purpose*," calling a bird of prey from the east, the man of my counsel from a far country. *I have spoken, and I will bring it to pass; I have purposed, and I will do it.*

God will bring His words to pass regardless of whether or not we can perceive how He will see it done.

We must always take Scripture in a straightforward way when

we interpret it. This is especially true when it comes to prophetic passages. Many Bible teachers of the past doubted that Israel would ever become a nation again. Instead of reading prophecy in a literal, straightforward way, they chose to spiritualize, symbolize, or outright ignore the prophetic passages. However, those who did take these prophecies literally were eventually vindicated.

I gave a presentation and wrote an article on this methodology to help explain and defend why we should approach prophecy in a literal, straightforward way. Since this was true of the prophecies concerning Jesus' first coming, why not His second coming?[2]

USING LOGICAL DEDUCTION TO UNDERSTAND PROPHECY

Before continuing on the topic of the coming third temple, let me provide one more example of how we can use logical deduction to understand end-time prophecy. For the last fifty years prophecy teachers have claimed that a cashless society would characterize the end times. Why would they make such a claim? While the Bible never explicitly predicts a "cashless society," these well-known verses describe something similar:

> Also it causes all, both small and great, both rich and poor, both free and slave, to be marked on the right hand or the forehead, so that *no one can buy or sell* unless he has the mark, that is, the name of the beast or the number of its name.
> —REVELATION 13:16–17, EMPHASIS ADDED

Bible teachers have deduced that for this system to be implemented, a cashless or digital type of currency will have to be used in order to track people and prevent them from buying or selling.

When prophecy watchers first discussed these verses with regard to a cashless society back in the 1970s, computer technology was in its infancy, and most people did not own a personal computer. Today they are ubiquitous around the world. We call them smartphones. They are minicomputers far more advanced and sophisticated than the government computers of the 1970s and '80s.

Most Americans might not realize this, but dozens of cashless communities already exist in China. These are 100 percent cashless, digital communities. If you do not have the proper app, you cannot buy or sell in these cities. You can read more about the extensive and advanced cashless technology of the Chinese government in two excellent books. One book, written in 2018 by Kai-Fu Lee, is called *AI Superpowers: China, Silicon Valley, and the New World Order*. The other, published in October 2022 by Martin Chorzempa, is titled *The Cashless Revolution*.

Most of the future advancements in cashless "progress" will come through corporations and not necessarily government legislation. This change is only the beginning for those living in America and the rest of the Western world. These digital technologies will help make Revelation 13:16-17 come true. Bible teachers understood this more than fifty years ago because they made a logical deduction from the text of Revelation. The same holds true for the third temple and the red heifer.

JESUS SPEAKS OF A PHYSICAL TEMPLE

We already saw that Daniel 9:27 proves that a third temple will be in existence in the time of the end. A second proof is found in the Olivet Discourse, given by Jesus Himself. In two places Jesus says something similar. Matthew 24:15 reads, "So when you see the abomination of desolation spoken of by the prophet Daniel, standing in the *holy place* (let the reader understand)" (emphasis added; see also Mark 13:14).

We find two similar occurrences of the phrase "holy place" in the Greek New Testament (Acts 6:13; 21:28). Both of these references in the Book of Acts refer to the temple. Therefore, Jesus, as a prophet, was giving us a snapshot of a future time period when an abomination will occur in the temple. Even though no temple exists today, we know that one will be built in the future in which the abomination of desolation will occur.

The "abomination of desolation" phraseology appears in the Book of Daniel (9:27; 11:31; 12:11) and in the apocryphal book of 1 Maccabees 1:41-59. Daniel 11:31 ("And they shall set up the abomination that makes desolate") and the Maccabees passage refer to an event that can only be interpreted as a real physical event that happened in the second century before Christ when the Seleucid king Antiochus IV entered the sanctuary in 167 BC and desecrated it by putting an idol on the altar mixed with pig's blood. According to Josephus:

> Now it came to pass, after two years, in the hundred forty and fifth year, on the twenty-fifth day of that month which is by us called Chasleu, and by the Macedonians Apelleus, in the hundred and fifty-third olympiad, that the king came up to Jerusalem, and, pretending peace, he got possession of the city by treachery....And when the king had built an idol altar upon God's altar, he slew swine upon it, and so offered a sacrifice neither according to the law, nor the Jewish religious worship in that country.[3]

According to Maccabees:

> On the fifteenth day of the month Chislev, in the year one hundred and forty-five, the king erected upon the altar of holocausts *the abomination that causes desolation*, and pagan altars were built in the surrounding towns of Judah.
> —1 MACCABEES 1:54, EMPHASIS ADDED

However, Daniel 9:27 ("on the wing of abominations shall come one who makes desolate") and 12:11 ("the abomination that makes desolate") both describe prophecies to be fulfilled at the end of the age. Jesus intimates that what happened during the Maccabean period was a prototype of what will happen again at the end of the age during the seven-year tribulation period. In order for the words of Jesus to be fulfilled, a third temple must be rebuilt. This is a logical deduction from the text of Scripture.

PAUL TEACHES ABOUT A PHYSICAL TEMPLE

A third passage that provides solid reasoning supporting the concept of a physical third temple is found in 2 Thessalonians 2. In it, Paul taught the Thessalonians extensively about the coming seven-year tribulation period known as the day of the Lord and the events leading up to its arrival.[4] (See also Isaiah 13:6-13; Joel 2:1-2; and Amos 5:18-20.)

The Thessalonians were confused and had likely read a false letter, allegedly from Paul, trying to convince them that the day of the Lord had arrived. Paul wrote his second letter to the Thessalonians to remind them of the order of events that he had previously taught them:

> Let no one deceive you in any way. For that day will not come, unless the rebellion comes first, and the man of lawlessness is revealed, the son of destruction, who opposes and exalts himself against every so-called god or object of worship, so that he takes his seat in the temple of God, proclaiming himself to be God. Do you not remember that when I was still with you I told you these things?
> —2 THESSALONIANS 2:3-5

Paul reminds the Thessalonian believers that the day of the Lord (the seven-year tribulation period) will start with the rebellion (apostasy) and the man of lawlessness (Antichrist) being revealed. I believe what Paul teaches is that the apostasy and revealing of the man of lawlessness actually marks the beginning of the day of the Lord (cf. John 5:43; Isa. 28:15). For the Thessalonians, neither of those events had happened, so they could not be living in the day of the Lord. I explain this further in appendix A.

Paul continues describing what the Antichrist will do after the day of the Lord begins. He will take his seat in the temple of God, proclaiming himself to be God. This desecration is synonymous with the abomination of desolation. Paul gave this prophetic snapshot at a time when the temple was still standing, but it was destroyed in AD 70. Many people probably wondered what to make of Paul's prophecy, since it was not fulfilled in the first century and could not be fulfilled without a standing temple.

We have been waiting for nearly two thousand years, but I emphasize, we must let the text mean what it says in a normal, straightforward, literal way. From where we stand today at the end of the age, we are watching the situation in Israel shift right in front of our eyes. Jerusalem is now under the sovereign control of

Israel. The United States embassy was moved to Jerusalem on May 14, 2018. Religious and political attitudes have changed dramatically in the last fifteen years, and we are seeing a convergence of various factors applicable to the building of the third temple—factors that did not exist even twenty years ago.

John Writes of a Physical Temple and Altar

The final passage giving reason to believe that a physical third temple will be rebuilt in the last days is found in Revelation 11:1-2:

> Then I was given a measuring rod like a staff, and I was told, "Rise and measure the temple of God and the altar and those who worship there, but do not measure the court outside the temple; leave that out, for it is given over to the nations, and they will trample the holy city for forty-two months."

John was catapulted in the Spirit and allowed to see the future (Rev. 1:10; 4:2; 17:3; 21:10). The Lord Jesus gave him several visions of the day of the Lord (seven-year tribulation), which He instructed John to write down and send to the seven churches of Asia Minor (Rev. 1:11).

John saw a snapshot of a physically rebuilt temple. The angel who spoke with John also bore witness to an existing temple and altar in the city of Jerusalem during the future day of the Lord. He told John to measure the temple of God and the altar. This same Greek word, *metreō*, is used in other portions of the Book of Revelation to measure something real and physical (21:15-17). Since the temple of God apparently exists in the future day of the Lord, we can deduce that it must be built prior to that time. It is quite reasonable to expect to see preparations being made to rebuild the coming temple as we see the end of the age quickly approaching.

Some people will argue that these passages refer to a nonphysical, spiritual temple such as the church, the body of Christ. No doubt Paul refers to the church as a "temple" in a few places. This has caused many well-meaning Christians to dismiss prophecies that refer to a coming, rebuilt third temple as misguided and irrelevant. I will address these arguments in the next chapter.

SOME IN THE EARLY CHURCH ANTICIPATED A REBUILT TEMPLE

Amazingly, we see evidence in the early church (approximately AD 30–400) that at least some of the church fathers read these texts in a normal, literal way. They recognized these passages as demonstrating that a new, third temple must be rebuilt in the future in order to see these passages fulfilled.

Jeffrey A. D. Weima writes in the *Baker Exegetical Commentary on the New Testament* on 2 Thessalonians 2:4,

> Some have understood Paul's reference here to the Jerusalem temple as grounds for believing that, in light of this temple's destruction in AD 70, it must be rebuilt at some time in the future so that it will be possible for the apostle's prediction about the man of lawlessness's blasphemous actions to take place. Thomas [in the *Expositor's Bible Commentary*] (1978: 322), for example, states: "This ['the temple of God'] is evidently a Jewish temple to be rebuilt in Jerusalem in the future" (this interpretation goes back all the way to Hippolytus in his *Treatise on Christ and Antichrist*, 25, paragraphs 6 and 63; and Cyril of Jerusalem in his *Catechetical Lectures*, 15.15).[5]

Hippolytus of Rome lived between AD 170 and 236. This is very early, but he believed and taught that the Antichrist would rebuild a temple of stone in Jerusalem and seek to rule from there: "The Saviour raised up and showed His holy flesh like a temple, and he will raise a temple of stone in Jerusalem. And his seductive arts we shall exhibit in what follows."[6]

Cyril of Jerusalem lived AD 313–386 and taught the same idea, that another temple would be rebuilt similar to the one that was destroyed in AD 70.[7] These two church fathers based their belief primarily on Paul's writing in 2 Thessalonians 2:4.

Recent, Pre-1948 Commentaries Predicted a Rebuilt Jewish Temple

It is important to take Scripture at face value when it comes to understanding prophecy. Even now we have the privilege of seeing prophecies come to fruition, which strengthens our faith. But as Jesus said, "Blessed are those who have not seen and yet have believed" (John 20:29). I think of William E. Blackstone, who in 1878 wrote his book *Jesus Is Coming*. He had tremendous faith and believed that the prophecies concerning the return of the Jews to the land and the rebuilding of the third temple should be taken literally.

Blackstone wrote concerning the Antichrist:

> He will be received, even by the Jews, who, having returned to their own land and rebuilt their temple, will make a treaty with him, called by the prophet "a covenant with death and an agreement with hell." And antichrist will exalt himself above all that is called God, or that is worshipped, so that he as God sitteth in the temple of God (the rebuilt temple at Jerusalem) and sheweth himself that he is God.[8]

What amazing faith Blackstone displayed by writing this in 1878, long before the Jewish people had any chance of establishing the State of Israel! He was confident that the third temple would be rebuilt because he believed the Scriptures were true, and so should we.

The Bible teaches that truth should be established by two or three witnesses (Deut. 19:15; Matt. 18:16; 2 Cor. 13:1; Heb. 10:28). God gave us four prophets—Daniel, Jesus, Paul, and John—to tell us that a future physical temple will be in existence at the time of the day of the Lord. But it will not be built in one day; we should not be surprised that it will be a process that involves many layers as well as people, money, and more to see it accomplished. The rest of this book will help explain how the steps being taken now are unprecedented and the actual building of the temple seems closer than ever.

WHAT ARE THE REQUIREMENTS FOR THE RED HEIFER?

We will explore many more details in subsequent chapters, but for now I will introduce the overall requirements for the red heifers as determined by modern rabbis who study the Hebrew Scriptures and their tradition.

The most important requirement for the red heifer—besides the obvious one, that it is a female cow—is that the cow has no blemish. A blemish is defined as having more than two non-red hairs in one single follicle. If that is found, the heifer is disqualified. Other requirements include that not a single physical blemish or spot should be found on the heifer, and it must never have been used for labor, including never having been harnessed or yoked. The heifer must never have been pregnant or used in a breeding program, nor even have been allowed to mate with a male cow. The heifer must be within its third year (at least two years and one month old). Finally, it must be slaughtered outside the holy city of Jerusalem but within sight of the third temple complex.

In summary, why should we care about the red heifer? The main reason is that today's Jewish rabbis believe that before the third temple can be rebuilt, they must find and procure at least one red heifer, then slaughter the animal and obtain the ashes necessary to be used for purification of the priests as well as the Temple Mount itself. I will discuss and explain this more fully in the subsequent chapters, but for now it is important to recognize that whether or not the Jewish people are correct in thinking they need the red heifer ashes, they are determined to obtain them.

In a later chapter we will discuss the implications of the red heifer as it relates to New Testament (New Covenant) theology. In the same way that we used logical deduction to determine that a third temple must be built, we will apply this reasoning to the importance of the search for the red heifer. (I discuss the biblical basis in the next chapter.) Thus, in the Jewish way of thinking, the red heifer is a prerequisite for the actual construction of the temple. Most if not all of the other preparations for the construction of the third temple are completed, but the acquisition of a pure red heifer has been the missing puzzle piece. All that is changing right before our very eyes.

The fact that the hunt for a pure red heifer seems to be coming to fruition reveals to us the prophetic importance of the third temple being rebuilt soon. Serious obstacles in the past have made the building of a third temple unfeasible. However, the religious, political, historical, logistical, and even archaeological circumstances have changed dramatically in the last twenty years, especially since the beginning of 2022. I will go into more detail about this in the remaining chapters, but next I want to address the confusing views many Christians hold concerning whether the New Testament prophecies speak of a physical temple or a spiritual temple.

Chapter 3

HANDLING OBJECTIONS TO THE EXISTENCE OF A PHYSICAL THIRD TEMPLE

MORE CHRISTIANS THAN you might expect reject the prophetic teaching that a third temple will be built. They typically base their objection on a narrow selection of New Testament verses that use "temple" verbiage in a metaphorical way. Let's examine our options and allow the grammatical, historical context and common sense to influence the proper interpretation for each of these alleged interpretations.

THE MEANING OF THE ENGLISH WORD *TEMPLE* IN THE NEW TESTAMENT

To begin with, we should simply examine the data. The two main Greek words used for *temple* in the New Testament are *hieron* and *naos*. The Greek word *hieron* is a general term for the physical temple building and refers to the entire complex, including the outer courts. However, *naos* is a specific term that refers to the temple building itself, which contains the holy place and the holy of holies.

Two of the texts we covered in chapter 2 (2 Thessalonians 2:4 and Revelation 11:1–2) both use the Greek word *naos*. We can infer from the Daniel 9:27 passage that there is a temple in existence due to the mention of sacrifices and offerings. When Jesus tells His disciples to watch for the abomination of desolation "standing in the holy place," He uses the Greek term *hagios topos* (meaning "holy place") to telegraph a physical temple spoken of by the prophet

Daniel. As discussed previously, the Greek word *naos* refers to the holy place inside the temple building itself.

The word *naos* is used more than forty times in the New Testament, and in only a few of these scriptures is it used in a metaphorical way.

Let's look at the ways the word *naos* (temple) is used in Scripture. It refers to the following:

- **The holy place inside the literal physical temple at Jerusalem**
  John wrote, "Then I was given a measuring rod like a staff, and I was told, 'Rise and measure the temple of God and the altar and those who worship there, but do not measure the court outside the temple'" (Rev. 11:1-2).

- **The physical body of Jesus as the "temple"**
  John wrote, "Jesus answered them, 'Destroy this *temple*, and in three days I will raise it up.' The Jews then said, 'It has taken forty-six years to build this *temple*, and will you raise it up in three days?' But he was speaking about the *temple* of his body" (John 2:19-21, emphasis added). In this passage it is crystal clear that Jesus uses the term metaphorically, as John clarified for us in verse 21.

- **The church as a "temple"**
  Paul wrote, "Do you not know that *you* are God's *temple* and that God's Spirit dwells in *you*?" (1 Cor. 3:16, emphasis added). The Greek word for *you* in this passage is plural and refers to the entire church at Corinth. In this case the local church functions as a temple of God in which the Holy Spirit dwells in a special way.

- **The physical human body of an individual believer as a "temple"**
  Once again, Paul wrote, "Or do you not know that

your *body* is a *temple* of the Holy Spirit within you, whom you have from God?" (1 Cor. 6:19, emphasis added). Paul's use of *naos* here is consistent with the way Jesus used it in John 2:19–21. Metaphorically, *naos* can be used to refer to the human body. This usage is rare, occurring only twice in all of the New Testament.

- **The church of God as the "temple"**
  We also read, "What agreement has the *temple* of God with idols? For *we are the temple* of the living God; as God said, 'I will make my dwelling among them and walk among them, and I will be their God, and they shall be my people'" (2 Cor. 6:16, emphasis added). This is another instance where *naos* is used to refer to the church of God.

- **The corporate body of Christ as a "temple"**
  The last occurrence of the metaphorical use of *naos* is written by Paul: "So then you are no longer strangers and aliens, but you are fellow citizens with the saints and members of the household of God, built on the foundation of the apostles and prophets, Christ Jesus himself being the cornerstone, in whom the whole structure, being joined together, grows into a holy *temple* in the Lord" (Eph. 2:19–21, emphasis added).

If we summarize all the various nuances of the forty times the word *naos* (temple) appears in the New Testament, we see it used in three different ways. This list comprises all of our options:

First, we observe the literal or normal use, referring to the physical temple building.

Second, we find the metaphorical use, referring three times to the church as the people of God and the figurative temple of God.

The third use is also metaphorical and is used twice to refer to the physical human body.

Understanding the Context

When it comes to the four passages that refer to a future third temple as spoken of by Daniel, Jesus, Paul, and John, we need to ask, "How is the Greek word *naos* (temple) used in these contexts?" Actually, we only have to look at two passages. Daniel is in the Old Testament and does not use the word *temple*. Rather, Daniel 9:27 speaks of "he" who puts an end to sacrifice and offering; the word *temple* is not used. In Matthew 24:15 when Jesus speaks about the abomination of desolation "standing in the *holy place*" (emphasis added), He is clearly referring to the physical temple. That should be enough to settle the issue, but in the interest of being thorough, let's address the final two uses by Paul and John.

Paul says that during the day of the Lord, the man of lawlessness "takes his seat in the *temple* of God, proclaiming himself to be God" (2 Thess. 2:4, emphasis added). How should we interpret this? Since the word *naos* is used, we have three options. First, this could be read in a straightforward and literal sense, referring to a newly rebuilt, physical third temple on the Temple Mount in Jerusalem in the future. Based on the context and most common usage of the word, this makes the most sense.

However, if we substitute the metaphorical use of number 2 from our list above into 2 Thessalonians 2:4, it doesn't make sense for the Antichrist figure to take his seat in the church. Which seat? Which church? How will he declare himself to be god in the church? Things become convoluted when we try to make this metaphorical use fit. By comparing the seating of the Antichrist in a physical third temple with Jesus' description of him being "in the holy place" in Matthew 24:15, it makes logical sense.

The "abomination that makes desolate" Jesus references from Daniel 12:11 could very well be the arrival of the Antichrist sitting in the holy place of a newly rebuilt third temple declaring himself to be god. However, if we plug in metaphor number 3 from our list above, which refers to the physical human body, this gets even more ludicrous. How could the Antichrist figure sit in the "temple of the human body" and declare himself to be god? This would require some very fanciful speculation and interpretation.

It seems quite obvious that the literal, physical temple of some sort offers the most straightforward interpretation of Jesus' description in Matthew 24:15. The Antichrist will sit in the physical, rebuilt temple of God in Jerusalem and commit an abomination by declaring himself to be god.

Next, let us look at how John uses the word *naos* in Revelation 11.

> Then I was given a measuring rod like a staff, and I was told, "Rise and measure the *temple* of God and the altar and those who worship there, but do not measure the court outside the *temple*; leave that out, for it is given over to the nations, and they will trample the holy city for forty-two months."
> —REVELATION 11:1–2, EMPHASIS ADDED

Use number 1 of a physical temple makes perfect sense here, especially since we are given other physical elements like the physical altar and the physical court outside the physical temple. John also brings up another physical description, that this newly rebuilt temple is in the holy city, which we know is Jerusalem. (See Daniel 9:24–27.) Was John asked to measure the local church (use number 2) or the human body (use number 3)? Clearly these metaphorical uses are quite foolish.

In conclusion, the Bible teaches that truth should be established by two or three witnesses (Deut. 19:15; Matt. 18:16; 2 Cor. 13:1; Heb. 10:28). God has given us four prophets—Daniel, Jesus, Paul, and John—as witnesses to show us that a future physical temple will be in existence at the time of the day of the Lord. But, again, it will not be built in one day but will require a process. The era of the Lord's return has arrived. Each area of prophecy is converging as we watch.

Chapter 4

THE RED HEIFER IN THE BIBLE

As students of the Bible, I imagine that all of us at one time or another have wished we had more details about the topics we find interesting. Having more specific information about the world before Noah's flood would help us understand ancient antediluvian history. A fuller explanation of the wheels within wheels in Ezekiel 1 would be much appreciated. How about the saints who were raised from the dead after Jesus' resurrection (Matt. 27:52–53)? Did they die again? Did they ascend with Jesus? Lord, can You please give us a little bit more information?

Yet God has reserved certain things to remain mysterious. Moses wrote, "The secret things belong to the LORD our God, but the things that are revealed belong to us and to our children forever, that we may do all the words of this law" (Deut. 29:29). When it comes to the slaughter of the red heifer, a few straightforward facts exist as well as some interesting conundrums written in the text of Scripture. For this reason, many books and articles have been written about the mystery of the red heifer. We will explore these mysteries in the coming pages.

Today's Jewish rabbis base their understanding of the red heifer ceremony on two main sources. The first is the biblical Book of Numbers, and the second includes the traditional sources of the Mishnah, Talmud, and the Midrash commentaries. We will look at the traditional sources and what they entail in the next chapter, but for now I want to start by examining the only place in the Old Testament where the red heifer ritual is mentioned.

We will examine the entire chapter of Numbers 19, paragraph by paragraph, with some commentary in order to gain an understanding of how Jewish rabbis interpret this text today. My goal is not to assess whether we should agree with their interpretations of the text; instead, I hope to show how the rabbis interpret and apply the text. Jewish rabbis have thousands of years of tradition influencing their opinions. Their interpretive traditions and thinking will determine how they approach the building of the third temple as well as how they believe the red heifer elements need to be included.

More importantly, what do Jesus the Messiah and His Father think about the building of the third temple? Do they approve of the efforts by the Jewish rabbis? A variety of opinions abound among modern prophecy teachers concerning these questions. I reached out to well-known prophecy teachers who were gracious enough to provide their thoughts. We will address their opinions in a later chapter.

THE RED HEIFER COMMANDMENT: NUMBERS 19:1–22

I find it fascinating that some Christians do not possess even a basic understanding of the red heifer. They may not realize the original commandment about the red heifer is found in the Bible.

Gordon J. Wenham, in his *Tyndale Old Testament Commentaries* on this chapter, provides a helpful introduction to the topic of uncleanness. He writes:

> Leviticus prescribes two methods of dealing with uncleanness: either washing in water and waiting till evening (11:28, 39–40; 15:16–18), or in more serious cases waiting seven days and then offering a sacrifice (14:10ff.; 15:13ff., 28ff.). Offering a sacrifice was a difficult and expensive procedure, which would have greatly added to the distress of family and friends when someone died. This chapter provides an alternative remedy which marked the seriousness of the pollution caused by death, yet dealt with it without the cost and inconvenience of sacrifice. Instead, those who have come in contact with the dead can be treated with a concoction of water that contains all the ingredients of a sin offering.[1]

Wenham does a great job of noting how coming into contact with a dead person was a reality that every person would eventually have to confront, and that God in His grace created an inexpensive way by which a person could become ritually clean after this happens. At the same time, God imparted valuable lessons into the process of slaughtering the red heifer, teaching His people that going from unclean to clean still required the death of an unblemished animal. A substitutionary sacrifice or slaughter involving blood was always needed for one to be forgiven (make atonement) or to become ritually clean (Lev. 17:11; Heb. 9:22).

Numbers 19:1–6

> Now the LORD spoke to Moses and to Aaron, saying, "This is the statute of the law that the LORD has commanded: Tell the people of Israel to bring you a red heifer without defect, in which there is no blemish, and on which a yoke has never come. And you shall give it to Eleazar the priest, and it shall be taken outside the camp and slaughtered before him. And Eleazar the priest shall take some of its blood with his finger, and sprinkle some of its blood toward the front of the tent of meeting seven times. And the heifer shall be burned in his sight. Its skin, its flesh, and its blood, with its dung, shall be burned. And the priest shall take cedarwood and hyssop and scarlet yarn, and throw them into the fire burning the heifer."

The original commandment, called a "statute of the law," was given to Moses and Aaron the high priest. The non-Christian Jewish scholar Jacob Milgrom wrote a commentary on the Book of Numbers for the Jewish Publication Society (JPS) in 1990 called *The JPS Torah Commentary: Numbers*, and in it he consults often with rabbinical thought. I took a course on rabbinic theology in college, and this commentary series was highly recommended to help us gain a solid grasp of how rabbis seek to interpret the Bible. I am not sharing this to endorse his work but to give you an opportunity to see how modern religious Jews interpret this passage.

The word *statute* (Hebrew *Chukat haTorah*, literally "This is the statute of the Torah") also appears in Numbers 31:21. We can see that the verbiage is tied to the ritual uncleanness caused by interacting with a dead body. This connection becomes very important later in rabbinic thinking concerning graves. There are thousands of graves, marked and unmarked, all around the Temple Mount area, including the Mount of Olives and possibly the Kidron Valley. We will examine later what the rabbis are implementing today in consideration of the potential uncleanness that could result from a priest walking over an unmarked grave during the ritual slaughter of the red heifer.

Another interesting thought concerning this phraseology is that Moses commanded the people of Israel to bring the red heifer to the high priest without outlining any stipulations about the location from which they were to obtain the cow. This becomes important when we discuss rabbinic traditions that had much to say about this. Did it need to be an Israeli cow raised in the land of Israel, or could it be purchased from Gentiles? The rabbis have an answer in their traditions, but the biblical text does not specify.

We learn from Milgrom that the red heifer was to be "without blemish, in which there is no defect."[2] This apparent redundancy is for the sake of emphasis. (See Leviticus 22:21 for the identical construction.) The rabbis, however, interpret "without blemish" as referring to the color: "unblemished red."

Milgrom writes, "Hebrew 'adom,' usually rendered 'red,' probably means 'brown' (for which there is no Hebrew word). Brown cows, of course, are plentiful, but one that is completely uniform in color, without specks of white or black or without even two black or white hairs, is extremely rare. Thus the rabbinic interpretation is preferred."[3]

We will see later that the rabbis are looking for cows that are redder in color rather than brown. Milgrom's commentary was first published in 1990, and a lot has changed since then.

Do not miss the specification that the heifer could never have been used for work or had a yoke on it. The rabbis took this to the extreme, seeking a heifer that had never had anything laid on its back. They said even a bird landing on the back of a cow could disqualify it! The Bible does not stipulate this, which illustrates the lengths to which the rabbis will go in adding their tradition.

It is also essential to note that the ritual slaughter had to take place outside the camp. In later biblical times when the temple was established by Solomon in Jerusalem, and even into the second temple period of the first century, we learn from rabbinic tradition that the red heifer was slaughtered and burned on the slopes of the Mount of Olives, which is east of the Temple Mount across the Kidron Valley. This is an unusual ritual in that the entire cow—including the drained blood—was to be burned. As the heifer was being burned, the priest was instructed to add cedarwood, hyssop, and scarlet yarn to the fire.

Interestingly, and with good reason, some people see a connection between the hyssop being used in the red heifer ritual and a hyssop branch being used to offer Jesus wine on the cross. "A jar full of sour wine stood there, so they put a sponge full of the sour wine on a hyssop branch and held it to his mouth" (John 19:29). This insight points the reader of the fourth Gospel back to the red heifer ceremony.

Numbers 19:7–13

> Then the priest shall wash his clothes and bathe his body in water, and afterward he may come into the camp. But the priest shall be unclean until evening. The one who burns the heifer shall wash his clothes in water and bathe his body in water and shall be unclean until evening. And a man who is clean shall gather up the ashes of the heifer and deposit them outside the camp in a clean place. And they shall be kept for the water for impurity for the congregation of the people of Israel; it is a sin offering. And the one who gathers the ashes of the heifer shall wash his clothes and be unclean until evening. And this shall be a perpetual statute for the people of Israel, and for the stranger who sojourns among them. Whoever touches the dead body of any person shall be unclean seven days. He shall cleanse himself with the water on the third day and on the seventh day, and so be clean. But if he does not cleanse himself on the third day and on the

seventh day, he will not become clean. Whoever touches a dead person, the body of anyone who has died, and does not cleanse himself, defiles the tabernacle of the LORD, and that person shall be cut off from Israel; because the water for impurity was not thrown on him, he shall be unclean. His uncleanness is still on him.

After the ritual slaughter, the priest was required to wash his clothes and bathe because he had become unclean. We learn from verse 8 that the high priest did not need to be the one performing the ceremony but simply had to oversee the procedures. One mystery of the red heifer ceremony is that the ritual of burning the ashes that later have the ability to cleanse people of uncleanness actually causes those performing the service to be unclean. This ritual is not only for Israel but for any foreigner who has chosen to live in Israel under the Mosaic covenant.

Once the ritual ceremony was completed, the ashes were to be kept safe. Milgrom writes, "To be kept, rather, 'to be safeguarded,' the ashes of the red cow must be guarded scrupulously lest they become invalidated through contamination. During second temple times the ashes were divided into three parts: one-third for sprinkling, one-third for sanctifying new lustral water, and one-third for safekeeping."[4]

God then gave Moses and the people of Israel specific instructions about how to mix the ashes of the red heifer with water in order to purify someone of uncleanness. The unclean person had to be sprinkled with the new water on the third and seventh days (v. 12). If the person did not follow this exactly, they defiled the tabernacle or temple of the Lord and would be cut off from the people of God. This was a very serious situation, and it is why God created the ceremony to produce the red heifer ashes.

Milgrom writes: "The demand for purification from corpse contamination was so great during Second Temple times that the purificatory waters were made available in twenty-four districts of the country. Even after the destruction of the temple these waters were still available in Judea, Galilee, Transjordan, and Ezion-geber (Assia) in the south."[5]

The Mystery of the Red Heifer

Numbers 19:14–22

> This is the law when someone dies in a tent: everyone who comes into the tent and everyone who is in the tent shall be unclean seven days. And every open vessel that has no cover fastened on it is unclean. Whoever in the open field touches someone who was killed with a sword or who died naturally, or touches a human bone or a grave, shall be unclean seven days. For the unclean they shall take some ashes of the burnt sin offering, and fresh water shall be added in a vessel. Then a clean person shall take hyssop and dip it in the water and sprinkle it on the tent and on all the furnishings and on the persons who were there and on whoever touched the bone, or the slain or the dead or the grave. And the clean person shall sprinkle it on the unclean on the third day and on the seventh day. Thus on the seventh day he shall cleanse him, and he shall wash his clothes and bathe himself in water, and at evening he shall be clean. If the man who is unclean does not cleanse himself, that person shall be cut off from the midst of the assembly, since he has defiled the sanctuary of the LORD. Because the water for impurity has not been thrown on him, he is unclean. And it shall be a statute forever for them. The one who sprinkles the water for impurity shall wash his clothes, and the one who touches the water for impurity shall be unclean until evening. And whatever the unclean person touches shall be unclean, and anyone who touches it shall be unclean until evening.

This section is straightforward and provided stipulations for what should be done when a person died inside a tent. This was a common occurrence, especially during the forty-year wilderness wandering during which that entire generation died off. In verse 17 we read about blending the water and the ashes of the red heifer in a vessel in order to create a mixture that could be sprinkled on the tent and persons.

Milgrom writes, "The text implies that the water was added to the ashes. The rabbis, however, held that the ashes were added to the water. Perhaps the ashes were held in a porous cloth through which the water was filtered."[6] This practice was important to the traditions of the rabbis. Because they chose to interpret the text as saying the ashes were added to water instead of water being added to the ashes in a vessel, they were able to exponentially expand the volume of mixed ashes and water available to be kept for the people. This also allowed them to create gigantic stores of the mixture that could be transported and kept continuous for generations.

As you can see from examining the biblical text, very specific stipulations are outlined, but an extensive number of regulations are not explained. The text does not get into the details of the why or even the how, but simply provides a general overview. It makes sense, therefore, that the rabbis spent so much time throughout the ages coming up with interpretations that made the nonexplicit explicit. They did not want to offend God, so they had friendly arguments back and forth about the extreme details, which I will cover in the next chapter.

ANTICIPATION OF THE DAY OF THE LORD

Why should we care about the nitty-gritty of rabbinic historical thought concerning the red heifer? One could argue that modern believers do not need to care much; the Bible says a third temple will be rebuilt, and that is all we should care about. That perspective might be satisfactory to some, but I have a different outlook.

God calls the day of the Lord a time of intense trouble.

> The great day of the LORD is near, near and hastening fast; the sound of the day of the LORD is bitter; the mighty man cries aloud there. A day of wrath is that day, a day of distress and anguish, a day of ruin and devastation, a day of darkness and gloom, a day of clouds and thick darkness, a day of trumpet blast and battle cry against the fortified cities and against the lofty battlements. I will bring distress on mankind, so that they shall walk like the blind, because they have sinned against the LORD; their blood shall be poured out like dust, and their flesh like dung. Neither their silver nor their gold shall be able to deliver them on the day of the wrath of the LORD. In the fire of his jealousy, all the earth

> shall be consumed; for a full and sudden end he will make of all the inhabitants of the earth.
> —ZEPHANIAH 1:14-18

Even more serious, God says through Jeremiah, "Alas! That day is so great there is none like it; it is a time of distress for Jacob; yet he shall be saved out of it" (Jer. 30:7).

The Jewish people believe that the earthly kingdom will come through the arrival of the Messiah. This is true, but before it does, God is going to have a serious talk with them about their rejection and killing of Jesus the Messiah. God will use the seven-year time of tribulation known as the seventieth week of Daniel, a seven-year period known as the day of the Lord, and the culminating day of the Lord to discipline Israel into a state of repentance and acknowledgment of their sin of piercing their Messiah. (See also Zechariah 12:10.)

We know that by the end of the tribulation, persecution will be so severe that the people of Israel will call upon the name of Jesus to rescue them from the Antichrist and worldwide persecution meant to bring genocide on the Jews. Jesus said that the Jewish people would not see Him again until they receive Him.

> O Jerusalem, Jerusalem, the city that kills the prophets and stones those who are sent to it! How often would I have gathered your children together as a hen gathers her brood under her wings, and you were not willing! See, your house is left to you desolate. For I tell you, you will not see me again, until you say, "Blessed is he who comes in the name of the Lord."
> —MATTHEW 23:37-39

This passage reveals that many religious Jewish people currently believe they need to build a temple to please God in order to draw closer to Him. To do this, they must also follow the prescriptions of Numbers 19 and perform the ritual slaughter of the red heifer in order to obtain the ashes and cleanse the Temple Mount area in preparation for the construction of the third temple.

The rabbis outlined extremely detailed specifications to make this happen. Some of these criteria are extremely difficult to re-create, but through His providence, God is allowing them to come to fruition. Why? Because God's ultimate goal is to save the Jewish people (Rom. 11:26).

God knows that in order to get the Jewish people focused on Him, they will need to slaughter the red heifer, build the temple, make an agreement with the false messiah (Antichrist), and then be put under serious distress, as Jeremiah 30:7 shows. Then and only then will their hearts be humbled to receive and call out to Jesus at the end of the tribulation period.

> I will return again to my place, until they acknowledge their guilt and seek my face, and in their distress earnestly seek me.
> —HOSEA 5:15

In the next chapter we will examine the finer details of rabbinic thought concerning the red heifer. We will also recognize that as extreme and stringent as these technicalities may be, the possibility that they could be fulfilled in our time appears to be likely after a hiatus of almost two thousand years. As outlandish as it seems to see the convergence of all these details in our day, it is all the more amazing to realize we are living in the time of their fulfillment!

Remember that the ultimate point of watching the time is not simply to be amazed at prophecy, but to ask yourself whether you are spiritually ready for the Lord to return at the rapture.

Chapter 5

THE RED HEIFER IN RABBINIC TRADITION

LET ME JUST say up front that this chapter serves as only a basic summary on the very wide and complex world of rabbinic tradition. Yet this discussion is necessary because the rabbis today who are seeking out and preparing for the slaughter of the red heifer continue to base their requirements not only on the Hebrew text of the Bible but also on the various traditions handed down to them over the past two thousand years.

As we ponder these prophetic developments, questions arise regarding the events we are observing in Israel today. The following questions are discussed in the rabbinical writings.

- What is the age requirement for the red heifer to be slaughtered?

- How many non-red hairs would disqualify a red heifer?

- In what specific location does the red heifer need to be burned?

- What if the red heifer is not born and raised in Israel? Can it be purchased from the Gentiles?

I have studied rabbinic theology for more than twenty years, and it can be quite laborious at times! If you are not that interested, feel free to skim the following survey. Not everyone is drawn into the minutia of the large body of literature known as rabbinic tradition. For those interested in the details, the following overview will provide original source material to which most people either do not have access or would not know where to look for it. There are many correlations between Jesus and the oral traditions, as well as other parts of the New Testament.

One of the best ways to learn more about rabbinic tradition is through the free basic edition of Logos Bible software. In the free edition you'll find *The Lexham Bible Dictionary*, which I highly recommend. In order to keep it simple and direct you to something you can check out on your own, the following is from that dictionary under "Rabbinic Literature and the New Testament," with my explanations in brackets.

OVERVIEW OF RABBINIC LITERATURE

The Jewish rabbis have two sources of authoritative texts. The first is the biblical text of the Hebrew Bible. It is often called the Tanakh, which is an acronym of sorts. The T is for Torah (the first five books of the Old Testament, written by Moses); the N is for *Nevi'im*, which is Hebrew for *prophets*; and the K is *Ketuvim*, meaning the writings. This gives us TNK, which with some vowels mixed in becomes *Tanakh*.

The second authoritative text is under the category of rabbinic literature and is often called the oral Torah. *The Lexham Bible Dictionary* states:

> Rabbinic literature is a body of literature composed by Jewish sages who examined the written Scripture in light of the oral Torah. These writings can broadly be divided into two parts:
> 1. literature centered on the law
> 2. literature dedicated to the theology and exposition of the Old Testament
>
> The part of rabbinic literature centered on the law is specifically focused on halakah [Jewish religious laws], and some of the texts in this part include:
>
> - the Mishnah [the oral Torah written down around AD 200]

- the Tosefta [similar to the Mishnah and seen as a supplement to it; written around the same time as the Mishnah]
- the two Talmuds: Yerushalmi (the Talmud of the land of Israel [finalized AD 350–400]) and Bavli (the Talmud of Babylonia [collated in Babylon and finalized AD 500])
- Exodus: Mekhilta

[The following are basically commentaries, in a general sense.]

- Leviticus: Sifra
- Sifré to Numbers
- Sifré to Deuteronomy

Some rabbinic works committed to the theology and exposition of the Old Testament include:

- Genesis Rabbah
- Leviticus Rabbah
- Pesiqta deRab Kahana
- Lamentations Rabbah
- Song of Songs Rabbah
- Ruth Rabbah
- Esther Rabbah[1]

The rabbis believe God gave Moses the written Torah, and we would agree. In addition, although there is no specific evidence that supports it in the biblical text, the rabbis remain steadfast in their belief that God also gave Moses the oral Torah, which is the proper interpretation of the written Word. This oral tradition is said to have been passed down through the various scribes, priests, and prophets from Moses in about 1400 BC all the way to around AD 200 when this oral tradition was finally written down by Rabbi Judah ha-Nasi in what is called the Mishnah.[2]

Jesus and the Oral Torah

We read in the New Testament that in the time of Jesus, the oral tradition, or the "tradition of the elders," was in existence. For a Jewish rabbi this tradition has just as much authority as the written Word of God. Christians and other Jews (known as *Karaite Jews*) do not believe the oral Torah or tradition carries the same level of absolute authority as the biblical canon. In the Gospels we see that Jesus referenced the tradition of the elders on several occasions. He never quoted it as an authority, and in some instances He rebuked the Pharisees for allowing their traditions to be held as equal with the written Word of God or even taking away from the written Word.

Mark the apostle writes:

> And the Pharisees and the scribes asked him, "Why do your disciples not walk according to the *tradition of the elders*, but eat with defiled hands?" And he said to them, "Well did Isaiah prophesy of you hypocrites, as it is written, 'This people honors me with their lips, but their heart is far from me; in vain do they worship me, *teaching as doctrines the commandments of men*.' You leave *the commandment of God and hold to the tradition of men*." And he said to them, "You have a fine way of rejecting the commandment of God in order to establish your tradition! For Moses said, 'Honor your father and your mother'; and, 'Whoever reviles father or mother must surely die.' But you say, 'If a man tells his father or his mother, "Whatever you would have gained from me is Corban"' (that is, given to God)—then you no longer permit him to do anything for his father or mother, thus making void the word of God by *your tradition that you have handed down*. And many such things you do."
> —MARK 7:5-13, EMPHASIS ADDED

Adherence to this tradition at times made it hard for the Pharisees to follow the written Word. The simple fact is that Jesus made a strong distinction between the written, authoritative Word of God and the nonauthoritative traditions of the elders.

Does this mean every part of the Jewish tradition is wrong? Not at all. In fact, most of their efforts were directed at keeping people from committing sin. Rabbis would take a well-known law of the written Word, such as the prohibition against adultery, and add new laws ("fences") around it to help keep a person from sinning.

These fences became part of the oral law, or traditions. For example, the Mishnah says in Kiddushin 4:12, "A man may not be secluded [alone] with two women lest he sin with them, but one woman may be secluded [alone] with two men."[3] It also says in Kiddushin 4:14, "Anyone who has professional dealings primarily with women may not be secluded [alone] with women."[4]

If you go to Israel today and interact with ultra-Orthodox Jewish men, you may see them be completely dismissive of a woman stranger in their presence. We might interpret this as being rude, yet for them the oral tradition gives the previous instruction, and so if they follow it, they will never commit adultery and break the written commandment. They have built a fence around the law. Think of it like a cliff, where falling off the edge represents committing adultery. If you build a fence twenty feet from the cliff and never cross it, you will never even come close to falling off (in this case, committing adultery). That is part of their logic.

The Mishnah and Talmud

The Mishnah (and Tosefta) are arranged with six major divisions called orders. These summations of religious oral law cover a variety of topics, including seeds (agricultural rules), festivals, women, damages, holy things, and purity laws. Each of these orders has many subchapters.

The Talmud as a body of literature can appear in printed editions up to thirty-eight volumes! It is huge, and one must complete a great amount of study to be fluent in it. The Talmud has two different editions, as mentioned previously: the Jerusalem (Yerushalmi) and the Babylonian. Both follow a similar organizational structure based on the Mishnah. These Talmuds have two parts. The first paragraph of a section is a reprinting of the actual text of the Mishnah (AD 200), and then what follows on the page is called the *Gemara*. The Gemara is a commentary and analysis of the Mishnah conducted by various rabbis up to around AD 400. The Talmud is thought to have been finished around AD 500.

When it comes to the ritual slaughter of the red heifer being prepared in our current day, the rabbis have consulted the Bible (Num. 19) and all the various traditions of the last two thousand years. Of the hundreds of topics that appear in the Mishnah, there is a specific chapter on the red heifer ceremony. In the sixth order there is a subchapter called *Parah*, which is the Hebrew word for *cow*. I cannot cover every last detail here, but I will mention a few that are important in our search to understand the prophetic implications of events that are happening in the present era.

Remember, these are exciting times! God is providentially allowing these events to come to pass in preparation for the arrival of the seven-year tribulation period and eventually the return of Jesus. Not one of these items is a coincidence. Though we must be spiritually prepared at all times, it seems like things have been moving extremely fast over the last few years and are continuing to accelerate.

Now that we have achieved a short summary of the rabbinical writings, we can revisit the original questions about the requirements for the red heifer stated at the front of this chapter.

- What is the age requirement for the red heifer to be slaughtered?

- How many non-red hairs would disqualify a red heifer?

- In what specific location does the red heifer need to be burned?

- What if the red heifer is not born and raised in Israel? Can it be purchased from the Gentiles?

WHAT IS THE AGE REQUIREMENT FOR THE RED HEIFER?

A well-known witticism says, "When two Jews are present, you have three opinions." This is so true that Jewish people often joke about this stereotype. It is also evident if you spend any time in the rabbinical writings. As we examine some of these questions in the rabbinical literature, we will realize that we cannot formulate definitive answers. Various rabbis give differing opinions and arguments for theological viewpoints. You can observe this in the following section of the Parah chapter from the Mishnah about how old the heifer should be.

1:1   A   R. Eliezer says, "A heifer—a year old.
       B   And a cow—two years old."
       C   1. And sages say, "A heifer—two years old, and a cow—three years old,
            2. or four years old."
       D   R. Meir says, "Even one five years old.
       E   1. The old one is suitable.
            2. But they do not keep it waiting, lest a hair turn black [and] it should not [otherwise] become unfit."
       F   Said R. Joshua, "I heard only *shelashit* {the third}."
       G   They said to him, "What is the meaning of the language, *shelashit* {the third}?"
       H   Said he to them, "Thus I have heard plain [without explanation]."
       I   Said Ben Azzai, "I shall explain.
       J   If you say *shelishit*, [it means the third in relationship] to others in sequence.
       K   And when you say *shelashit*, [it means] three years old."

1:2   A   R. Yose the Galilean says, "Bullocks—two years old.
       B   As it is said, *And a second [year] bullock of the herd you take for a purification offering* (Num. 8:8)."
       C   And sages say, "Even one three years old."
       D   R. Meir says, "Even one four years old,
       E   even one five years old are suitable.
       F   But they do not bring old ones, because of the honor [of the altar]."[5]

As you can see in this quote from the actual Mishnah text, rabbis through the centuries have various opinions. Some say the heifer should be one, two, three, four, or even five years old. So what is the final opinion? In Israel today, religious factions often disagree with each other. Even among the ultra-Orthodox Jewish groups you will find varying commentary and judicial requirements.

As I mentioned earlier, Rabbi Chaim Richman of the Temple Institute, who is still active and considered the premier authority in the matters of rebuilding the temple, wrote a book called *The Mystery of the Red Heifer*. In that book he mentions that Rabbi Eliezer, an esteemed rabbi of the first and second centuries who was quoted in the previous Mishnah text, believed the red heifer needed to be two years old. Yet Rabbi Richman says that Rabbi Meir's judgment of three years old is the consensus accepted by the majority of the rabbis today. However, how one defines three years old also is debated.[6]

The well-known ancient Targum Pseudo-Jonathan, an Aramaic translation of the Pentateuch, translates Numbers 19:2 this way: "This is the decree, the publication of the law which the Lord hath commanded, saying: Speak to the sons of Israel, that they bring to thee from the separation of the fold a red heifer, *two years old*, in which there is neither spot nor white hair, on which no male hath come, nor the burden of any work been imposed, neither hurt by the thong, nor grieved by the goad or prick, nor collar (band) or any like yoke."[7] This passage provides another ancient source of understanding that a two-year-old heifer is the appropriate age. Nevertheless, the modern rabbinic consensus has a divergent view.

THE CURRENT CONSENSUS

What does this mean for our current situation? There have been several potential red heifers through the years. Since the 1990s, several candidates started out as good possibilities and were later disqualified by growing non-red hairs. The consensus ruling comes into focus when discussing the five red heifers from a ranch in Texas that were flown to Israel and landed on September 15, 2022. These heifers were born around October 5, 2021.

This date is important considering the prophetic significance of the time when they will become eligible to be slaughtered. Even though we know the relatively close birth date of this group of five red heifers, there is still confusion about how old the prophesied red heifer must be according to Jewish tradition. In my research, I have heard from credible sources that the rabbis believe it needs to be at least two years and eight days old, and up to three years and eight days old. The present consensus is two years and one month old (the third year).

These conclusions became quite important when the five red cows from Texas came of age in November 2023. Boneh Israel—a nonprofit group that I will describe in more detail a bit later—planned to perform the ceremony during Passover of 2024 (April 5-13, 2024) or during the fall festivals in 2024. However, due to geopolitical events that I will address later, neither of these came to fruition.

The Temple Institute has stated quite vocally that even if these current five heifers do not qualify at the proper age, they have arrangements with several ranchers who are breeding other red heifers to send to Israel. Additional breeders are also breeding red heifers inside the land of Israel. They have not and will not give up trying to fulfill this requirement for the building of the third temple.

How Many Non-Red Hairs Will Disqualify a Heifer?

In the same way there are differing opinions about the required age of the red heifer, there are also various opinions among rabbinical tradition and literature regarding how many non-red hairs would disqualify a red heifer. The Bible teaches that it must be a red cow but does not give exact specifics as to what that means. This is where rabbis through the centuries have sought to make explicit what was not made explicit in the text of Scripture. Their opinions are recorded in the Mishnah and the Babylonian Talmud. Notice, first, the varied opinions as conveyed in the Parah chapter of the Mishnah:

> **2:5** A [If] there were on it two black hairs, or white ones, inside a single follicle, it is unfit.
> B R. Judah says, "Even in one hollow."
> C [If] they were in two hollows, and they are opposite [adjacent to] one another—it is unfit.

> D R. Aqiba says, "Even four, even five, and they are scattered about—let one uproot them."
> E R. Eliezer says, "Even fifty."
> F R. Joshua b. Beterah says, "Even one on its head and one on its tail—it is unfit."
> G There were on it two hairs—
> H their root is black and their head is red—
> I their root is red and their head is black—
> J "All follows that which is seen," the words of R. Meir.
> K And sages say, "[All follows the condition of] the root."[8]

We find similar discussions and ambiguity in the Talmud. Parah 2:7A-E of the Talmud Babylonia reads:

> O. If there were on a red cow two black hairs or white ones in one follicle, it is unfit; in two follicles—it is fit. R. Judah says, "Even in two follicles and they are adjacent to one another, it is unfit." If there were on it two hairs, with a red root and a black head, R. Yosé b. Hammeshullam says, "One shaves the top and does not reckon with the possibility that he is liable on account of shearing the red cow."[9]

As you can read, a single consensus is not reached in either the Mishnah or the Talmud. Some rabbis even say it is permissible to pluck out some of the non-red hairs in order to maintain that it is keeping its red color.

The Temple Institute website has published several articles pertaining to the red heifer. They write:

> The heifer must be three years old and perfect in its redness. This means that the presence of as few as two hairs of any other color will render it invalid; it is related that for this reason, the red heifer was always very expensive to procure. Even its hooves must be red. It must also be totally free from any physical blemish or defect, whether internal or external.[10]

The Temple Institute is *the* leading organization to determine what is accepted in the Jewish community. By their standards even two non-red hairs from a single follicle would disqualify the cow, while others say two non-red hairs are OK. I imagine more will be revealed as we get closer to the date.

MAIMONIDES SPEAKS ABOUT THE RED HAIR

Maimonides (1138–1204), the twelfth-century rabbi and scholar whom I introduced in chapter 1, wrote a massive, fourteen-volume tome called the *Mishneh Torah*, which was a treatise on Jewish law. The *Mishneh Torah* drew upon various influential Jewish writers from the time of the Talmud (AD 500) up until his own time. His opinions carry great weight today, and I include them here for easy access.

Maimonides gave his opinion on the back-and-forth decisions concerning how many non-red hairs are allowed on the red heifer. His writing leans toward a commonsense approach, in that the most important determining factor is whether the roots of the hair are red.

Maimonides wrote this more than one thousand years after the second temple had been destroyed. He longed for the time when the temple would be rebuilt and set out to provide a framework for this to happen. The following is from chapter 1 of his book on the red heifer. (You can find the full text at chabad.org; search for Parah-Adumah, chapter 1.) He writes:

> Included in this text are two positive commandments. They comprise the following:
>
> 1) the laws of the red heifer; 2) the laws of the impurity and purity brought about by the water used for the sprinkling of its ashes. These mitzvot [commandments] are explained in the ensuing chapters.
> 1. The commandment involving the red heifer is to offer such an animal in its third or fourth year of life. If it is older, it is acceptable, but we do not wait for it to age longer, lest its hairs become black.

The Jewish community does not purchase a calf and raise it, for Numbers 19:2 states: "And you shall take unto yourselves a heifer," i.e., a heifer, not a calf. If only a calf was found, a price is established for it and it should remain in its owner's possession until it matures and becomes a cow. It should be purchased with money from the Temple treasury.

2. The Torah's description of this heifer as "perfect" means "perfectly red," not perfect in stature. Even if it is dwarfsize, it is acceptable, as is the law regarding other sacrifices. If it had two white hairs or black hairs growing from one follicle or from two cavities and they are lying on top of each other, it is unacceptable.

3. If there were two hairs, their roots reddish and their heads blackish, or their roots blackish and their heads reddish, their status follows the roots entirely. One should cut off the blackish head with scissors. He need not be concerned about the prohibition against shearing consecrated animals, because his intention is not to shear.

4. Enough of the red hair must remain so that it can be pulled out by tweezers. For if a hair is not large enough to be pulled out by tweezers, it is considered as if it does not exist. Therefore if there were two white or black hairs that are so small that they cannot be pulled out by tweezers, it is acceptable.

5. If its horns or hooves are black, they may be cut off and it is acceptable. The color of the eyeballs, the teeth, and the tongue do not disqualify a heifer.[11]

The important thing to note is that, once again, the final conclusion as to how many non-red hairs will be accepted could change. Strong opinions are held by various groups, and each group has its cherished ancient source on which to appeal. Depending on how desperate the situation becomes, the consensus could easily change based on legitimate sources in their scholarship and traditions.

Where Does the Red Heifer Need to Be Slaughtered?

Regarding the specific location where the red heifer slaughter needs to take place, the short answer is on the Mount of Olives, which is east of the Temple Mount and across the Kidron Valley of Jerusalem. This detail alone reminds us that we are living in the age of fulfilled prophecy, with even more prophecy to come.

Israel became a nation in 1948 and gained control of eastern Jerusalem—which includes the Mount of Olives—in 1967. Without these miraculous historical events it would be impossible to prepare for the building of the third temple or the slaughter of the red heifer.

There is no question as to where the slaughter of the red heifer took place. The Mishnah says it quite clearly in the Parah chapter:

> **3:6** A And they would make a causeway from the Temple mount to the Mount of Olives, arches upon arches, an arch directly above each pair,
> B because of the grave in the depths,
> C on which the priest who burns the cow, and the cow, and all those that assist it go forth to the Mount of Olives.[12]

I encourage you to check out the Temple Institute's website and its pages on the red heifer at templeinstitute.org/red-heifer-the-ceremony. You'll find beautiful artistic renderings of the entire ceremony as well as information about the priests and the other regulations. As we read above in the Mishnah, there was a causeway from the Temple Mount across the Kidron Valley to the proper location of the ritual slaughter. This causeway is illustrated at the Temple Institute website. In the picture, and as written in the Mishnah, it is noted that the causeway was held up by arches. This relates to rabbinic thinking concerning graves.

We saw earlier from Numbers 19:16–18 that God instructed that anyone who came into contact with a dead person or a grave would become ritually unclean. The rabbis took this literally and sought to find ways to make sure a priest would not become unclean if he inadvertently walked over an unmarked grave. How could they guarantee this? There were two main considerations. One would be to always walk on bedrock. The nature of bedrock would inherently prohibit the possibility that a grave could exist under the bedrock. The second was that if you built an elevated path with empty space between the elevated walkway and the ground, you would not become contaminated, as there is a separation of empty space between the ground and the walkway.

For this reason, the Mishnah records that the causeway built from the Temple Mount had arches. The use of an arched causeway guaranteed that priests could not become contaminated or unclean by coming into contact with a grave as they made their way from the Temple Mount to the location of the ritual slaughter of the red heifer. We see this reasoning in the Mishnah (quoted previously) and also later in Maimonides' teachings. He writes in chapter 3 of the *Mishneh Torah* about the location:

> 1. The red heifer should be burnt only outside the Temple Mount, as Numbers 19:3 states: *"And you shall take it outside the camp."* They would burn it on the Mount of Olives. A ramp was built from the Temple Mount to the Mount of Olives. Below it were arches upon arches, i.e., an arch on two arches, so that there would be empty space under it, lest there be a grave in the depths of the earth. Similarly, the place where the heifer was burnt and the place of immersion on the Mount of Olives had the space under them hollowed, lest there be a grave in the depths of the earth. The red heifer, the one who would burn it, and all those who assist in its burning go from the Temple Mount to the Mount of Olives on this ramp.
>
> 2. How was the red heifer burnt? The elders of Israel would walk to the Mount of Olives first. There was a *mikveh* there. The priest, those assisting in burning it, and the heifer would go out on the ramp and come to the Mount of Olives.[13]

The Modern Mount of Olives Connection

When it comes to the modern era, we can learn more about what rabbis have been doing to prepare for the slaughter of the red heifer. We learned in the preceding section that the slaughter must take place on the Mount of Olives and in line of sight with the temple building. This means that for the line of sight to be maintained, the location must be up on the slope of the Mount of Olives to a certain degree rather than down in the Kidron Valley.

Boneh Israel is a nonprofit organization in Israel. Their website describes their purpose as follows: "Boneh Israel (literally: 'Building Israel') is a nonprofit organization focused on building up and reviving important Biblical sites, bringing the Bible to life, educating the nations about the past, present and future of Israel, and actively bringing the redemption closer."[14] I had an opportunity to interview Byron Stinson, the American leader and advisor of Boneh Israel.[15]

In 2011, Boneh Israel purchased property on the Mount of Olives northeast of the Church of All Nations, where people can visit the Garden of Gethsemane. Currently this property is the main site that Boneh Israel and the Temple Institute are promoting as the location of the ritual. On the following map you can see the location of the property where they had planned to perform the ritual slaughter in spring of 2024.[16]

Another proposed site on the map is just west of and below the Dominus Flevit Church on the slopes of the Mount of Olives. This piece of property has an excellent line of sight with the Temple Mount and is a good candidate for the location of a future red heifer burning ceremony.

Joseph Good is a Gentile believer who teaches the Bible from a rabbinic perspective. He is well connected in Israel and with the Orthodox Jews. Based on information he presented on his Facebook page, Good believes this property near the Dominus Flevit church is one possible option for the location of the ritual slaughter of the red heifer.[17]

The Red Heifer in Rabbinic Tradition

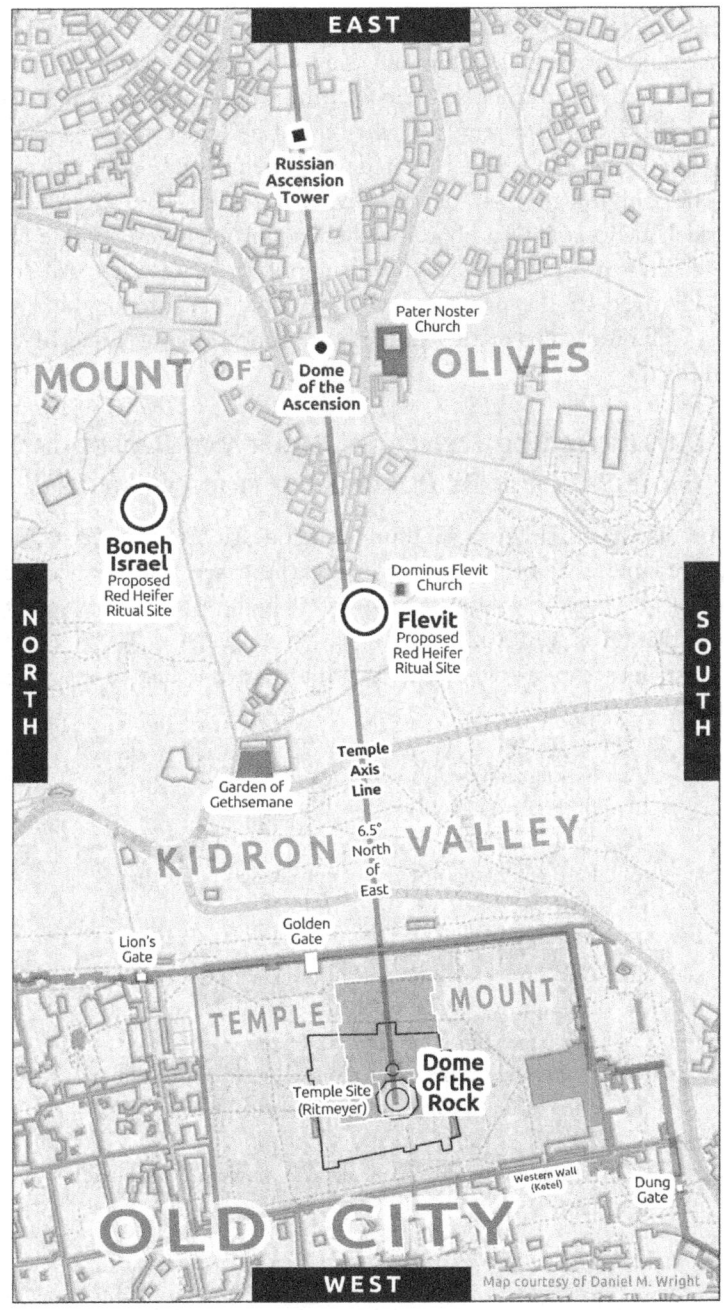

It is easy to see that many of the puzzle pieces are coming together. Things are converging before our eyes, with details being arranged and secured in advance so that all hindrances to performing the ritual will have been removed when a red heifer becomes available. Not that long ago, these recent developments were only a dream. Think of living in 1947 or 1966 when religious Jews around the world had no concrete hope for their vision of a new temple and the reinstitution of a red heifer slaughter to be realized. All that has changed in the present day. As Arnold Fruchtenbaum, PhD, says, "The footsteps of the Messiah are indeed being heard in our current day!"[18]

MUST THE RED HEIFER BE BORN AND RAISED IN ISRAEL? CAN IT BE PURCHASED FROM GENTILES?

Some fascinating history surrounds the question of the red heifer's required place of origin. In addition, there are uncanny connections and events involving the five red heifers that were sent to Israel from Texas in 2022.

First, let's explore what the Mishnah (Parah) has to say about this question.

2:1   A   R. Eliezer says, "A cow for purification which is pregnant is suitable."
        B   And sages declare unfit.
        C   R. Eliezer says, "It is not purchased from the gentiles."
        D   And sages declare fit.
        E   And not this alone, but:
        F   All community and private offerings derive from the Land and from abroad,
        G   from what is new and from what is old [produce],
        H   except for the *omer* and two bread [loaves, Lev. 23:17],
        I   which come only from what is new and from the land.[19]

This passage in the Mishnah quotes Rabbi Eliezer, who rules that the red heifer cannot be purchased from Gentiles. However, this is not the consensus today. Maimonides addressed this issue, writing in *Mishneh Torah* 1:7: "All of the physical blemishes that disqualify sacrificial animals, also disqualify a red heifer, for the prooftext cited above states: 'Which does not possess a blemish.' If the heifer was born by Caesarian section, was exchanged for a dog, was a present given a prostitute, was *treifah*, or had been sodomized, it is unacceptable. For any factor that invalidates a sacrificial animal for the altar invalidates the red heifer even though it is considered only as consecrated for the upkeep of the Temple, for Scripture has called it a sin-offering. *It is permitted to purchase a red heifer from a gentile.* We do not suspect that the gentile sodomized it, for he would not destroy the value of his animal."[20]

The general consensus today allows for the red heifer to be purchased from Gentiles, which is evident based on the fact that the five red heifers that arrived in Israel on September 15, 2022, were purchased from a rancher in Texas for a significant amount of money. I will share some interesting details about the modern story, but before I do, I will introduce a fascinating story in the rabbinic tradition discussing this exact question.

The Jerusalem Talmud, among other rabbinical literature, notes how a Gentile was praised for his honor to his father while he was sleeping. This story is found in Kiddushin (Qiddushin) 1:7.

> **2:3** A To what extent does the requirement of honoring the father and mother extend?
>
> B He [Eleazar, Y. Pe. 1:1] said to them, "Are you asking me? Go and ask Damah [son of] Netinah. He was the chief of the *patroboule* of his town. One time his mother was slapping him before the entire council, and the slipper she was beating him with fell from her hand, and he got down and gave it back to her, so that she would not be upset."
>
> C Said R. Hezekiah, "He was a gentile from Ashkelon, and head of the *patroboule* of his town. Now if there was a stone on which his father had sat, he would

never sit on it. When [his father] died, he made the stone into his god."

D One time the Benjamin's jewel in the high priest's breastplate was lost... *They said, "Who has one as fine as that one? They said that Damah [son of] Netinah had one. They went to him and made a deal with him to buy it for a hundred denars. He went to get it for them, and he found that his father was sleeping [on the box containing the jewel].*

E *And some say that the key to the box was on the finger of his father, and some say that his foot was stretched out over the jewel cask.*

F *He went down to them and said, "I can't bring it to you." They said, "Perhaps it is because he wants more money." They raised the price to two hundred, then to a thousand. Once his father woke up from his sleep, he went up and got the jewel for them.*

G *They wanted to pay him what they had offered at the end, but he would not accept the money from them. He said, "Shall I sell you [at a price] the honor I pay to my father? I shall not derive benefit by reason of the honor I pay to my father."*

H How did the Holy One, blessed be he, reward him?

I Said R. Yosé b. R. Bun, "That very night his cow produced a *red cow*, and the Israelites paid him its weight in gold and weighed it [for use for producing purification water in line with Num. 19:11ff.]."[21]

What can we learn from this story? Actually, we see how several aspects have shaped the thinking of many rabbis today.[22] Two details in particular stand out. The first is that the ancient Jews were looking to restore the jewel representing the tribe of Benjamin that was missing from the breastplate of the high priest. Second, they went to a Gentile man to buy the jewel, and he showed great honor to his father. In reward for honoring his father, God blessed this Gentile with a red heifer cow, which he also sold to the Israelites to fulfill their need.

I will share more details about the five red heifers flown to Israel in September of 2022 later in the book, but keep in mind that the owner of the ranch who sold these cows is a Christian man named Ty Davenport. He owns and runs Triple Creek Ranch (triplecreekredangus.com). Interestingly, his brother, Brian Davenport, was very instrumental in connecting the Israeli rabbis with his rancher brother. Why is this interesting? Well, would you believe that Brian Davenport is a diamond jeweler who has traveled to all parts of the world, including Israel, to sell jewels?

You can see why the rabbis are extremely excited. They approached a jeweler, who in turn introduced them to his brother, from whom they were able to acquire five red heifers. The narrative bears great similarity to the traditional story of Damah ben (son of) Netinah. What does this prove? Nothing, exactly. But it is one more story that includes some uncanny similarities and coincidences. Minute elements like these lead the rabbis to believe that God is guiding their steps toward procuring a red heifer to hasten the building of the third temple.

Does God really approve of the rabbis' efforts? Is God helping them find a red heifer? I will address this topic in a subsequent chapter, but I bring this up to illustrate how rabbis are interpreting these events. They are convinced that God is working out these little miracles and giving providential provision to support their efforts to acquire a red heifer.

The Appearance of a Tenth Red Heifer Heralds the Messiah's Arrival

There is one last rabbinic belief that I believe is worthy of being discussed in this chapter. Based on the previous story and several others, many rabbis are convinced that we are living in the age of the Messiah's arrival. And so are we as prophecy watchers! However, there is a big difference between what Christians believe will happen at the end of the age and what the Jewish rabbis believe.

As Christians, we believe that Jesus will come a second time to rapture His church, judge the world, and chasten the nation of Israel. We believe He will return on the clouds in full glory to destroy the Antichrist and his system, and then establish His thousand-year Messianic kingdom after redeeming a repentant Israel.

The religious Jews indeed believe that the Messiah will come, but to them this will be the Messiah's first appearance. They believe He will establish the Davidic kingdom, provide a red heifer, and build the third temple to restore the Mosaic covenant and its sacrificial system.

The Mishnah, written around AD 200, records a history of how many red heifers had been slaughtered since the time of Moses. It reads:

> **3:5** A "[If] they did not find [the residue of the ash] from seven [former cows of purification], they did it from six, from five, from four, from three, from two, from one.
> B "And who prepared them?
> C "The first did Moses prepare. And the second did Ezra prepare.
> D "And five from Ezra onward," the words of R. Meir.
> E And sages say, "Seven from Ezra onward.
> F "And who prepared them?
> G "Simeon the Righteous and Yohanan the High Priest did two each. Elyehoenai b. Haqqof and Hanamel the Egyptian, and Ishmael b. Phiabi did one each."[23]

Maimonides also contributed to the discussion when he wrote in the *Mishneh Torah* 3:4:

> Nine red heifers were offered from the time that they were commanded to fulfill this mitzvah until the time when the Temple was destroyed a second time. The first was brought by Moses our teacher. The second was brought by Ezra. Seven others were offered until the destruction of the Second Temple. *And the tenth will be brought by the king Mashiach;* may he speedily be revealed. Amen, so may it be G-d's will.[24]

This belief has become quite common, in that the religious Jews believe the time of the Messiah's arrival is close. They will not lock themselves into saying that only the Messiah can offer the red heifer as a ritual slaughter, but they do maintain that if a qualified red heifer were to arrive, it would be a sign heralding the soon return of the Messiah.

This is important because it means if a red heifer passes all the qualifications and is actually slaughtered, the religious Jewish mindset is poised and eager to receive someone as the Messiah. In subsequent chapters we will discuss the reasons why the religious Jews will accept the Antichrist as their Messiah. New Testament Christians know him to be a false deceiver, but many Jews will be blinded by their eagerness to build the third temple (John 5:43).

THE RABBIS DESIRE TO RETURN TO THE LAW OF MOSES

Next, I want to provide select ancient sources in addition to the biblical text explaining why and how religious Jews believe a red heifer slaughter should be carried out. As Christians the biblical text is our sole authority, but we must recognize that the religious Jews are quite adamant about including their traditional sources, which they consider authoritative, when deciding the required elements of the red heifer slaughter ceremony. The fact that many of their traditions are being fulfilled will also play a role in convincing them that God approves of their desire and mission to slaughter the red heifer, rebuild the third temple, embrace the "Messiah" (the Antichrist), and seek to reinstate the Law of Moses.

I will address more about this belief in a later chapter, but for now we must remember that for the religious Jews to go back to embracing the Law of Moses is not righteous in God's eyes. To do so is blasphemy and an outright apostasy against God and the work of His Son, Jesus the Messiah. If they truly followed the Law of Moses as they claimed, they would embrace Jesus.

> Do not think that I will accuse you to the Father. There is one who accuses you: Moses, on whom you have set your hope. For if you believed Moses, you would believe me; for

he wrote of me. But if you do not believe his writings, how will you believe my words?

—JOHN 5:45–47

See also the Book of Hebrews, which argues for the supremacy of Jesus over the temple rituals, which only served their God-given purpose until Jesus arrived. Since Jesus has been offered as the final sacrifice, their efforts to restore the Mosaic system are no longer honorable to God.

Even though the biblical text has not changed, and the Mishnah and Talmud have been locked in for more than a thousand years, the current era of religious Judaism shows signs of accepting modifications to some of their traditional viewpoints. As we saw in this chapter, oftentimes multiple opinions exist on a single topic. This means rabbinic groups can reorient their "conclusions" by revisiting the divergent opinions found in their traditions. In the next chapter, I will address some ways in which the current atmosphere in modern Israel has been changing among the rabbis and within the government of Israel itself.

Chapter 6

Rabbis' Changing Views in Recent Years

I CANNOT SAY IT enough: We are living in exciting times! All the perspectives taught by prophecy teachers for the last 150-plus years are now approaching maturity in our current time. I have been watching prophecy for thirty years, and I shouldn't say that I am shocked at how fast prophetic developments are accelerating today, but I am! Shocked is not the best word; it is thrilling to see all these signs and events begin to converge.

I have always believed these prophecies to be true, but to actually see them happen in my time and in surprising ways is exhilarating. It takes me back to the theological viewpoints before 1948. So many godly theologians at that time could not believe that Israel would ever become a nation. Some even admitted that when they read the biblical text at face value, it revealed that Israel would somehow return as a nation, but instead of interpreting it in a straightforward, literal way, they looked at the events of their own day through their human thinking, adapting a spiritual or allegorical method to explain their current situation. This is folly, and we should not repeat this error.

While we do not have all the information as to exactly how events will play out, we are seeing things mature every week. We no longer need to turn to speculation or conjecture; we can see things happening. This should give us prophecy watchers even more reason to lean into the Lord, stay faithful, evangelize, and be ready for the Lord's return!

Two items have changed recently regarding the construction of the third temple and the slaughter of the red heifer. The first change relates to how the religious Jews view their own presence on the Temple Mount. The second is how quickly the politics in Israel can change and affect prophetic developments.

Rabbis' Changing Views About the Temple Mount

The first item that has changed relatively quickly in the last thirty years is how rabbis view the Temple Mount. As I discussed in the first part of this book, after the Jewish army secured the Temple Mount for Israel in the Six-Day War, there was a short time of rejoicing that Jerusalem had finally been reunited. That initial rejoicing was followed by a long status quo period during which the religious rabbis ruled that Jews were forbidden to go up on the Temple Mount for fear of contributing to the desecration and uncleanness of the area where the holy temple once stood.

The rabbis' ruling was determined in the absence of a red heifer slaughter or the potential discovery of an ancient cache of red heifer ashes from the first century. Since neither of these have occurred, the rabbis have shown even more concern for preventing the contamination of the Temple Mount. This is why many religious Jews pray at the Western Wall (called the *Kotel* in Hebrew). Most refuse to go up on the Temple Mount but instead seek to pray outside the complex or along the Western Wall tunnels, which get you closer to what is believed to be the location of the holy of holies of Herod's temple. According to the traditional consensus viewpoint, they need the red heifer ashes in order to be cleansed and qualify to ascend to the area of the ancient temple without fear of desecrating it.

The website 972mag.com offers independent journalism from Israel-Palestine and provides an excellent overview of the recent change in many rabbis' perspective about the status quo presence of Jews on the Temple Mount. A March 2023 article written by Nate Orbach titled "The Temple Mount Movement Braces for Its Moment" provides tremendous insight. The following is a quote from this article:

> Finally, under the post-1967 status quo, Jews were permitted entry to the Temple Mount only under tightly controlled

conditions that included an express prohibition on prayer and ritual objects, and highly restricted hours of entry and points of access. This status quo was enforced by the Waqf, the Muslim religious authority that oversees the site; the Israeli police; and Muslim volunteers from two groups, the Murabitun (for men) and the Murabitat (for women), who would shout at and disrupt Jewish visitors, regarding their attempts to pray as a violation of the status quo and an infringement on an Islamic holy site.

Taken together, these obstacles kept the Temple Mount out of the minds of most Jews. Though multiple Temple Mount groups were founded in the years after 1967, they failed to gain much traction: the site remained, for most Israelis, irrelevant, dangerous, and forbidden.

By the 1990s, however, as the Oslo Accords took shape, rabbinical unanimity on the prohibition on Jews ascending to the compound began to crack, and the Temple Mount movement kicked into gear. Though the Oslo process deferred final status negotiations on Jerusalem until later stages, both Israel and the future Palestinian state were expected to claim the city as their capital, potentially sharing sovereignty in the Old City (or even handing over control to an international body, like the UN).

The prospect of giving up further land for peace—which had previously set off drastic rebellions among religious Jewish settlers during earlier peace talks, including a plot to blow up the Temple Mount in the early 1980s by the Jewish Underground terrorist group—provoked a sense of crisis for the expansionist wing of the religious-Zionist movement, and they understood this as their moment to stave off the Oslo catastrophe.

Religious-Zionist leaders in West Bank and Gaza settlements formed the Council of Yesha Rabbis and, after initially calling on Jews to ascend to the Temple Mount, contravening centuries of halachic rulings, announced that visiting the site was not only permissible but should be encouraged by rabbinic authorities.[1]

As you can see, fascinating developments are taking place among religious Jews today. This is not an accident. Just thirty years ago there was a pretty standard consensus among religious Jews to feel compelled by the rabbinic ban to not go up on the Temple Mount. According to an article by Judah Ari Gross on the *Times of Israel* website,

> The first crack in the consensus on the ban came in 1996, when the rabbinical council of the West Bank published a ruling that deemed it permissible to go up to the Temple Mount and encouraged rabbis who agreed with this view to do so with their congregants. In 2000, one of the co-founders of the Temple Institute, Rabbi Yisrael Ariel, released his own ruling that went further, arguing that visiting the Temple Mount was necessary to fulfill the biblical commandment of conquering the land of Israel, which meant that ascending the mount was not only permissible but required under Jewish law.[2]

Now, various groups are competing for the hearts and minds of the religious Jews in encouraging them to break the historic rabbinic consensus and ascend the Temple Mount complex itself. As of September 6, 2024, a record 51,672 Jews have visited the holy site since the previous Rosh Hashanah (September 16, 2023), according to the Beyadenu—Returning to the Temple Mount organization. The previous record was set just the year before when 48,144 Jewish people ascended the Temple Mount. The year before also had a record number, and it is becoming quite clear that the trend will likely continue.[3]

Fervor continues to build in the ethos of these modern movements. The Jewish people believe and feel that the arrival of the Messiah is coming soon. We Christians agree, but we also know that their view of the Messiah is far different from the true biblical view of Jesus as the fulfillment of Old Testament prophecy.

Today, three main groups have been increasing the pressure and public outcry to give Jews equal access to the Temple Mount. You can learn more about the various movements at templeinstitute.org, templemountfaithful.org, and thirdtemple.org.

Attitudes are changing regarding Jews being prohibited from ascending the Temple Mount. It started becoming more apparent in the 1990s and has now become an overwhelming resistance to the rabbinic prohibitions for Jews to ascend on the Temple Mount complex. In fact, many religious Jews are encouraging other religious Jews to simply ignore the rabbinic prohibitions. This is the first time in my thirty years of watching prophecy that this level of religious fervor for the Temple Mount is becoming mainstream.

Political Parties Are Shifting and Becoming More Religious

The second and biggest challenge since the 1967 takeover of eastern Jerusalem and the Temple Mount has been the political situation. In chapter 2 I wrote of how Moshe Dayan gave religious control back to the Waqf only seven days after the Six-Day War ended. Since the establishment of the modern State of Israel, the largest political parties have been relatively irreligious and socialistic.

Many religious groups have tried to change the status quo for the Temple Mount, and Israel's government has been their main impediment. From a practical and political standpoint this made good sense. The majority of Israel's politicians are secular or simply culturally Jewish and do not feel the same level of religious commitment or the need to see a temple rebuilt, deciding that upsetting the status quo would not be worth the likely conflict. As a result they have instead sought to reduce tensions with Muslims over Temple Mount claims, a position that has helped Israel maintain relative peace and harmony through the decades.

This attitude changed dramatically beginning in about 2010 and up to the current political environment and party makeup. The Israeli Knesset (parliament) is made up of 120 seats. Israel's multiparty system differs greatly from the American system. In the Israeli system, the majority (sixty-one seats) makes the decision in selecting the prime minister. However, no single party has ever won more than fifty-six seats. Instead, different parties must unite and form a coalition in order to secure the sixty-one seats required to appoint a prime minister from one of the coalition groups.

In the past, the religious groups were always in the minority and often ignored because the secular parties had enough seats in their coalition to make up the majority. Netanyahu has been the longest serving prime minister in Israeli history. He served one term from 1996 to 1999 by creating a coalition with centrist and religious parties. His second term (2009-2013) consisted of a mixed group of secular and religious groups. His third term (2013-2015) was also a mixed group. Netanyahu's fourth term (2015-2020) was again a mixed group of secularists and religious.

Netanyahu's government dissolved, and from May 2020 to June 2021 he shared a government with Benny Gantz, a secular centrist. This was followed by the more centrist and secular Naftali-Lapid government from June 2021 to November 2022. The numerous elections in these years brought significant turmoil and frustration for the average Israeli voter. In November 2022, Netanyahu once again formed a government, but this time he was only able to do so by joining with mostly religious parties. In December 2022, the officially formed government became recognized as the most religious government in the history of modern Israeli politics.

This new government brings significant changes to the political landscape of Israel. Netanyahu now leads a group of sixty-eight majority seats, which means the only way he was able to regain power in the first place was to cater to many of the demands of these religious parties. For the first time in the history of Israel, the religious and orthodox parties hold the greatest governmental influence over the Temple Mount, settlements, relations with the Palestinians—and most specifically, the idea of building a third temple.

Before we discuss the potential change to the status quo of the Temple Mount, I want to reference a recent article that discusses how the new religious government could bring significant changes to the Israeli court system.

Currently, Israel has a typical secular judiciary similar to what any democracy might have (the civil courts). However, sanctioned rabbinical courts are given full authority over marriages and divorce when both people are Jewish. A civil marriage is not an option for two Jewish people. In addition, the rabbinical courts have the authority to determine the authenticity of religious conversions. This has caused serious issues for Jews or Israelis who become followers of Jesus.

A special report article titled "Torah First: The Judicial Revolution No One Is Talking About" was published January 12, 2023, on Shomrim.com. The author, Chen Shalita, writes:

> Israeli headlines have been dominated by the proposed legal reform of Justice Minister Yariv Levin, but below the radar, buried deep in the coalition agreements, Likud has agreed with its partners to enact an equally dramatic revolution, which would split the Israeli judicial system and grant rabbinical courts the same powers as any other court. "You don't need to be an expert to recognize that there's more chance now of the legislation being passed."[4]

I am not offering an opinion on whether this is a good thing or a bad thing per se, but we do know that as we get closer to the seven-year tribulation period, religious influence will increase to such a degree that a third temple will be built. The growing religious fervor and political influence we are now witnessing is evidence that the tribulation period is inching closer and closer. This also means that the rapture is even closer!

CHANGING STATUS QUO OF THE TEMPLE MOUNT

Drawing our attention back to the Temple Mount, before the new Israeli government officially began operating, various articles were published to demonstrate how the new, very religious government could seek to change the status quo of the Temple Mount and cause conflict with the Palestinian and Jordanian groups.

One article in the *Times of Israel* is representative of that great concern. In the article, dated November 6, 2022, and titled "Fire on the Mount? How the New Government Might Shift Policy at Flashpoint Holy Site," author Jeremy Sharon wrote about far-right National Security Minister Itamar Ben-Gvir and others in his Otzma Yehudit Party who are longtime advocates for increased Jewish prayer rights at the Temple Mount. The article states that "activists hope they'll come through on promises."[5]

In January 2023, not long after that article was published, Ben-Gvir ascended to the Temple Mount to challenge the general status quo. Ben-Gvir is a devout, ardent religious Jew and has publicly stated that the discrimination against Jewish prayer on the Temple Mount should be stopped. Ben-Gvir organized a conference titled "Return of Israel to the Temple Mount" on July 24, 2024, at the Israeli Knesset. At this event he again advocated for a nondiscrimination policy on the Temple Mount.

According to an article in the *Jewish National Syndicate*, Ben-Gvir said that if it were up to him, he would build a synagogue on the Temple Mount. He further argued that current Israeli law does not prevent Jews from praying on the contested site. Israeli President Isaac Herzog expressed his "unequivocal commitment to preserving the status quo at the holy site—in accordance with political agreements laid down since 1967 [with Jordan], and in the spirit of the rulings by leading rabbis and religious figures over the last 100 years."[6] Prime Minister Benjamin Netanyahu has expressed similar sentiments.[7]

It will be interesting to watch Ben-Gvir's political career and observe whether he continues to gain influence or loses it. He has a notable career but has also been rather unfriendly to Christian believers. Back in July 2015, a group of religious Jews set fire to the Benedictine Church of the Multiplication of the Loaves and Fishes, severely damaging the church. The defense lawyer for the perpetrators—one of whom was convicted and sentenced to four years in prison—was none other than Itamar Ben-Gvir.[8] Assaults on and persecution of Christians living in Israel have increased, and many believe that as security minister, Ben-Gvir has done little to hold those criminals accountable for their actions.

Along this line of thinking, Christians have expressed a growing concern over the increased ultra-Orthodox element in the Israeli government and amplified hostility toward evangelical Christians. Author Joel Rosenberg recently wrote a public appeal to Prime Minister Benjamin Netanyahu, saying, "Specifically, the Ministry of Interior—currently led by Minister Moshe Arbel, an ultra-Orthodox rabbi and Knesset Member who is part of the religious Shas political party—has stopped issuing clergy visas for staff working at the International Christian Embassy Jerusalem (ICEJ) and similar Christian Zionist groups."[9] This was later reversed, but things could likely change at any moment depending on which majority parties are in power.

Netanyahu understands and appreciates the value of the evangelical Christian community's support for the nation of Israel. So far, it appears that some in the ultra-Orthodox government factions do not share the prime minister's perspective.

Another example of the current government becoming more public in its advocacy for a change in the status quo of the Temple Mount happened in June 2023. Knesset member Amit Halevi of the Likud party proposed a plan under which authority over the Temple Mount would be shared: the Muslims would control the southern end of the thirty-seven-acre site, and the Jews would gain control of the central and northern areas. These sorts of pronouncements are likely to increase under this new Israeli government.

Ben-Gvir joined in and visited the Temple Mount in July of 2023, during the Tish B'Av annual fast day, a day of remembrance that the destruction of both Jewish temples happened on the ninth day of the month of Av. Two other Knesset members joined Gvir on his Temple Mount visit and called for increased control. They were quoted as calling it "the holy place of the people of Israel" and said, "On this day, more than ever—may we be granted complete redemption and the building of the Temple soon in our days, Amen!"[10]

These are just a few examples of how the political mood is changing regarding the Jewish people's right to access and pray on the Temple Mount. Much could happen in the coming months and years, but the overall attitude is shifting. These events provide more evidence that we are entering the era of convergence: not only are the religious Jews changing their tune, but the political winds of change are also blowing, increasing the likelihood that the ritual slaughter of the red heifer and the building of the third temple are coming together.

I want to disclose one last piece of remarkable information concerning the politics of Israel. I had the opportunity to interview prophetic minister Robert Mawire, of WRNO Worldwide shortwave radio, in December 2022 at his office near Fort Worth, Texas. Mawire is well known in Israel for his philanthropic efforts and for helping to modernize the city of Ariel, Israel. The State of Israel conferred an award on Mawire for his contributions to the advancement of Israel society.[11] He has had several interactions with Prime Minister Netanyahu over the last twenty years, and the two are on a first-name basis.

During our interview, Mawire discussed his last conversation with Netanyahu. The prime minister told Mawire that after much prayer, he personally felt it was his destiny as a leader of Israel to be the prime minister who finally sees the third temple rebuilt. I was not there to hear this myself, but Mawire gave me permission to share this information and declared its authenticity, as he heard it personally. It is clear that since Hamas attacked Israel on October 7, 2023, and publicly referenced the "red cows" in January 2024, Netanyahu has distanced himself from the third temple rhetoric. Nevertheless, the voices have become more prominent and numerous.

Could this be another example of how God is shaping the political mindset in Israel to see the third temple rebuilt so Jesus can return? We can only wait and see as we watch the various elements mentioned in this chapter coming to fruition. In fact, the slaughter of the red heifer and the actual construction of the third temple are the last remaining items to be put into place before legitimate, religious sacrifices can be reinstated in Jerusalem.

In the next chapter we will explore other preparations that have been completed and are waiting for the temple to be rebuilt. All these preparations make for great conversation starters and demonstrate just how much prophecy is being fulfilled in the present time. I believe God ordained this well in advance to help us make the most of every opportunity and share with people that the end of the age has arrived. We must encourage others to be ready to meet the Lord Jesus at any time!

Chapter 7

The Pre-Temple Preparations

Because the Jewish leadership rejected Jesus as their Messiah in the first century, Jesus predicted that judgment would come upon that generation (Matt. 11:16; 12:39, 41-42, 45). In addition, when Jesus entered Jerusalem on Palm Sunday, instead of rejoicing over Jerusalem, He wept over it. He predicted that Jerusalem, and many of the people in it, would be destroyed because they did not recognize Him (Luke 19:41-45; 21:20-25).

We know that in AD 70, Jesus' words came true, and many Jews were exiled or killed. Another revolt took place in AD 132-135 under a man named Simon Bar Kokhba. After Rome defeated him, they expelled all Jews from the city of Jerusalem under pain of death and renamed the city Aelia Capitolina.

Since those times, religious Jewish people everywhere have been praying the Amidah prayer three times per day. This invocation consists of nineteen blessings, two of which refer to the regathering of Israel and the restoration of Jerusalem. Many groups include an addendum to this prayer, specifically asking for the third temple to be rebuilt. We observe this at the end of the Passover seder when people declare, "Next year in [rebuilt] Jerusalem." The longing for a restored Jerusalem with the third temple as its central focus has been in the hearts and minds of religious Jews since the first century, when the second temple was destroyed.

We can take comfort in knowing that God is the sovereign Lord of history. He is providentially working His prophetic plan, regardless of the schemes of wicked mankind. This includes the desire of His covenant people to build the third temple. As we saw in the introduction, God predicted that a third temple would be rebuilt, but only according to His perfect timing—at the end of the age, before His Son, Jesus, returns to set up His eternal kingdom. As I will show, God in His providence thwarted all previous attempts because it was not the proper prophetic time.

HISTORICAL EFFORTS TO REBUILD A THIRD TEMPLE

The first effort to rebuild the temple came under the Roman Emperor Hadrian (AD 117-138). Hadrian granted the Jewish people permission to rebuild the temple, but after preparations were started, he received a slanderous report from the Samaritans, causing him to stop the forward movement of reconstructing the temple. This eventually led to the Bar Kokhba revolt (AD 132-135), which was crushed by the Romans and interrupted the building of the temple.[1]

The second attempt was short lived and instigated by the Roman Emperor known colloquially as Julian the Apostate (AD 361-363). At the age of twenty, Julian, the nephew of Constantine the Great, abandoned his Christian upbringing with the goal of reintroducing paganism to the Roman Empire. Part of this process involved encouraging the Jews living in the land of Israel to rebuild and restore their temple sacrifices. He even offered tax exemptions and other incentives to finish the temple. Some Jews were eager to accept these offers, but factions between the priestly lines and the rabbis created an overall ambivalence toward accepting help from a pagan ruler. Additionally, some sources say that miraculous fires and earthquakes prevented the work from continuing unabated. Julian died within two years of his ascendancy to the position of emperor, and the dreams of a rebuilt temple once again faded.[2]

The third, short-lived attempt to rebuild the temple occurred early in the seventh century under the last pre-Islamic Iranian imperial dynasty (House of Sasan), known as the Sassanid Empire. The Sassanid military conquered the land of Israel in AD 610 and removed Christian rulership.[3] In the absence of Western Byzantine (Christian) governance, the Jews seized the opportunity and attempted to restart the practice of sacrifices. This did not materialize, as the Muslims entered the area around AD 630 and controlled the region for more than 1,300 years, which prevented any substantial and long-term efforts to rebuild a Jewish Jerusalem or a third temple. It was not until Israel recaptured east Jerusalem after the Six-Day War of 1967 that the people could place realistic hope in seeing their dream of a future temple fulfilled.

The Modern Third Temple Movement

In modern times, three main groups have been actively seeking and preparing for the building of the third temple. After the situation changed on the Temple Mount after the Six-Day War, the first group to begin their efforts called themselves the Temple Mount Faithful. The group started in 1967 and was originally led by Gershon Salomon, who died in November 2022.

A second and more recent group is the Third Temple Project, a consortium of various organizations worldwide dedicated to the rebuilding of the third temple. Their excellent website, thirdtemple.org, categorizes the efforts involved, including legal efforts, architecture, politics, construction, education, and media. They also have an interactive "Guided tour of the Temple Mount."

The third and most well-known organization is the Temple Institute, founded in 1987 (templeinstitute.org). Their website is replete with stunning pictures and illustrations of various preparations being made for the coming temple. They have done extensive work in crafting and preparing every conceivable object needed for a fully functioning sacrificial system. The following table lists all the implements they have fabricated. You can view most of these items on their website or even visit their museum in Jerusalem to see the items.[4]

ITEM	FUNCTION
Golden menorah (lampstand)	Used to light the inside of the holy place
Menorah cleaning vessels	Used for maintenance of the golden menorah
Oil pitcher	Holds the olive oil for the menorah

Small golden flask	For individual lamps of menorah
Table of showbread	Where the weekly bread for the priests is stored
Altar of incense	Where the special incense fragrance burns
Frankincense censer	Associated with incense offering
Incense chalice	Associated with incense offering
Incense shovel	Associated with incense offering
Ark	Holds stones of testimony
Sacrificial altar	Courtyard altar for sacrifices
Golden crown (inscribed with "Holy to the Lord")	Worn only by the high priest
Complete priestly garments	Very specific clothing worn by the high priest
Harp	Used in Levitical worship teams
Lyre	Used in Levitical worship teams
Silver trumpets	Used in a variety of ceremonial functions
Gold-plated shofar horn	Primarily blown during the feast of Rosh Hashanah
Silver-plated shofar horn	Associated with days of fasting
Silver cup for the water libation	Used for annual feasts
Silver libation vessels	Used for annual feasts
Silver shovel	Special shovel for the courtyard altar
Silver wine libation vessel	Used in offerings involving wine
Copper laver	Used by priests for various washings
Copper wash basins	Used by priests for various washings
Copper vessel for meal offerings	Used for various offerings
Small mizrak	Vessel that holds blood of animals being prepared for offering

Large mizrak	Vessel that holds blood of animals being prepared for offering
Pronged fork	Used with altar sacrifices
Measuring cup	Used to measure meal offerings
Crimson dye	Used in association with the red heifer ceremony
Lottery box	Used in association with Yom Kippur
Sickle	Device used to harvest the omers of barley
Abuv	A stand used to roast the omer of barley

The Temple Institute YouTube page has a playlist of three videos listed as "Holy Temple Building Plans" in which they animate walk-throughs of the coming third temple.[5] Over $100,000 was spent on architectural plans, and much of that design can be seen in those animations.[6] They are well worth checking out.

Rabbi Aryeh Lipo has been organizing and preparing stones in advance of the day that the government grants official permission to begin construction of the third temple. These stones are cut with tools, but once they are brought up to the Temple Mount area, no tools are allowed to be used to form them.[7]

In addition to the utensils and vessels mentioned in the chart, preparations are also being made for the music to be used in the anticipated temple worship services. Ariel Louis, who lives in Israel, is making handcrafted Baroque flutes from wood that is at least eighty years old.[8] Louis' late father, Rabbi David Louis, was commissioned by the Temple Institute to compose specific music for future celebrations. You can read more about these preparations at Israel365News in an article titled "What Is the Last Secret to Be Revealed Before the Messiah?" written by Adam Eliyahu Berkowitz.[9]

In addition to the priestly garments that have been meticulously crafted, priests (*kohanim*) are being trained to perform their services in a completed temple. The Kehuna Academy provides free online classes with the purpose of uniting and equipping any and all who qualify as priests. In 2020, freelance journalist Rivkah Lambert Adler wrote a full report about a number of priests who have been in training and will be ready when the time comes.[10]

I saved one final newsworthy development that I can finally reveal. When I interviewed Byron Stinson in the fall of 2023, he communicated to me in confidence that a major development had taken place related to the building of the third temple. Yitshak Mamo, a rabbi involved in the latest red heifer acquisition,[11] was asked by Prime Minister James Marape to travel all the way to Papua New Guinea. (Of special note is that Papua New Guinea is a large producer of gold.) When Mamo arrived and met with the Christian prime minister, Marape informed him that the government of Papua New Guinea had agreed to provide all the gold needed for the coming third temple! We read in the Hebrew Bible that Solomon overlaid the entire inner temple and other items with pure gold (1 Kings 6–7).

Once again, the timing of all these events and the way things are coming together seems to indicate that the time for the red heifer ceremony and the construction of the third temple is drawing closer each and every day.

Ceremonial Aspects of the Red Heifer Ritual

One particular ceremonial aspect of the red heifer ritual involves children. In ancient times, children would be seated on animals and led to the pool of Siloam, where they would let down buckets to retrieve the fresh, living water from the pool, which flows from the Gihon spring. They would ride the animals and take this water up to the Mount of Olives, where it would be mixed with the ashes of the red heifer.

Today, a group of children are being prepared for this service. The children were born in a complex built on solid bedrock. As we discussed earlier, walking on bedrock ensures that a person is not walking on any sort of grave, which would result in the person being contaminated. So, these children have been born and raised in a situation where they have always been on bedrock and thus are guaranteed to be ritually clean. They will be involved in the future red heifer ceremony. This is just one more layer of preparation being fulfilled in our generation.[12]

It is becoming a challenge to keep up with all the actions and training of the various priests and people in preparation for the coming temple. In October 2022, more than six hundred Levites joined together in a worship service rehearsal on the southern steps of the Temple Mount. Also in recent times, water libations and Shavuot grain offering ceremonies have been performed near the Temple Mount. These liturgical rehearsals were unheard of at this level before 1967.

According to rabbi Yitshak Mamo in a report from the Christian Broadcasting Network (CBN), the Temple Institute currently has nine pure priests.[13] This means they were not born in a hospital and have never traveled to places where they could have been contaminated by a grave or touching a dead person.

We are truly living in exciting times, as these events point to the quickly approaching day when our Lord Jesus will return to catch away His church!

A Red Heifer Bonfire Rehearsal

In closing, one more event worth mentioning happened in August 2019 and was reported by Adam Berkowitz on Israel365News. Zohar Amar, a professor in the department of Land of Israel studies at Bar-Ilan University, has long been interested in taking a scientific approach to the biblical text. For the first time in modern history—and maybe longer—someone in the land of Israel decided to perform a practice test of burning a cow with the intention of following the stipulations as outlined in the Bible and rabbinical writings.[14]

Professor Amar kept exact records of the amount of wood used in the ritual slaughter along with how many kilograms of ash was left after burning the 270-kilogram (594-pound) cow and the wood. It was reported that he did not use a red heifer but instead a sick adult cow.[15]

In preparation for the fire, a rectangular pit was carved into the bedrock approximately 14 feet long, 6.5 feet wide, and 3 feet deep. Inside this trough they built a pyre of pine and oak wood for the fuel. They slaughtered the cow, then lifted it onto the pyre. Once ignited, the fire reached a whopping 940 degrees in just over two hours. To burn the cow and all the wood took nine hours. It then took a few days for the ashes to cool down enough to be collected and measured. The total remaining amount of ash, including 11 kilograms (about 24 pounds) from the animal itself as well as the ashes from the wood portion, ended up being 145 pounds.[16]

According to the requirements, this ash was then mixed with spring water. The final conclusion was that each gram of ash could be added to 1,000 liters of water. From the yield of 145 pounds of ash, this experiment proved to be enough for 660 billion sprinklings! What this ultimately means is that even though several current red heifer candidates exist at the moment, one cow would be enough for many generations (or possibly centuries) of sprinkling. This amount would also be sufficient to cleanse the entire Temple Mount area in preparation for the construction of the third temple.[17]

In the next chapter we will explore the various efforts and historical searches for a qualified red heifer. The search has not been going on long, but several endeavors preceded the latest arrival of the five red heifers from Texas.

Chapter 8

THE MODERN SEARCH FOR THE RED HEIFER

WE LEARNED IN a previous chapter that the medieval rabbi Maimonides recorded that two red heifers were slaughtered by Moses and Ezra followed by seven more up until the second temple was destroyed in AD 70. He also stated around AD 1200 that the final, tenth red heifer to be slaughtered would herald the Messianic era. Once Israel became a nation and Jerusalem (including the Temple Mount) was in the hands of the Jewish people, at least superficially, a greater interest and focus grew concerning the forgotten dream of rebuilding the temple.

THE EARLY SEARCHES (1980s–2020)

The study of prophecy in the modern church age became of greater interest and influence with the publication of *The Late Great Planet Earth* by Hal Lindsey in 1970. This book had sold more than 28 million copies by 1990,[1] and those twenty years of influence had a direct bearing on the search for the red heifer. As we will see, several evangelical Christian ranchers developed a love for Israel and for seeing prophecy fulfilled. They were also aware that the Jewish people needed to procure a red heifer in order to provide cleansing ashes not only for a future priesthood but also for the Temple Mount proper, where a temple would hopefully be erected.

In his book about the red heifer, Rabbi Chaim Richman describes his first experience with these evangelical Christians who came to Israel in the spring of 1990 to visit the Temple Institute and gain more firsthand information about the requirements for the sacrificial red heifer. One of these individuals was Reverend Clyde Lott of Canton, Mississippi. As Clyde had been studying Genesis 30 in the previous year, he began to ponder how he could help develop a specific breed of red cow.

Over the next few years and after several trips to Israel, Clyde Lott and Rabbi Richman developed a plan to "help bring about a livestock and agricultural restoration throughout the land of Israel."[2] In the early 1990s they were instrumental in helping the cattle industry of Israel increase its efficiency and knowledge. One of their goals was to encourage the cattle infrastructure to focus on breeding red heifers that one day could be used in preparation for the coming temple.

The first real moment of excitement came on November 11, 1994, when Rabbi Richman traveled to Clyde's Mississippi ranch to examine four red heifers. After an extensive examination, Rabbi Richman declared one of them to be preliminarily qualified as the first red heifer candidate in two thousand years.[3]

As I discussed earlier, a qualified red heifer can become unqualified by growing more than two non-red hairs out of a single follicle and becoming blemished, or for other reasons. As cows get older, they often grow out of their younger hair colors. Eventually that first red heifer was disqualified. As Thomas Ice, PhD, executive director of the Pre-Trib Research Center, states in chapter 10, another cow named Gula from an American rancher was a candidate at one time, but it also later became disqualified.

Despite these initial disappointments, the Temple Institute has not given up on its efforts to establish ranches in the land of Israel dedicated to breeding and raising red heifers on Israeli soil. Other groups have joined in the establishment of procedures, processes, and ranches to facilitate the search for a red heifer fully qualified for the ritual slaughter.

My friend Jeff Van Hatten has been keeping an eye on the developments for decades. He has a website called raptureparty.net with a lot of prophetic content. He writes concerning the red heifer search:

> The Temple Institute had identified two candidates, one in 1997 and another in 2002, both initially thought to have met the requirements, but later found each to be unsuitable.

The headlines read: *"Apocalypse Cow"* in *The New York Times* (1997) and *"News Flash: Red Heifer Born in Israel"* in a Temple Institute web posting (2002). In 2014 the headlines read *"Torah-Condition-For-3rd-Temple-Now-Met,"* and articles reported that the Temple Institute had posted a video showing what appeared to be a perfect red heifer that was being raised at an unidentified location in the United States. A report from Right Side News said a "qualified" red heifer has not been seen in Israel for nearly 2,000 years....

In 2015, the Temple Institute in Jerusalem established a breeding program called *"Raise a Red Heifer in Israel"* to raise the necessary items needed for purification of the Temple and its priests. Israeli law does not allow the importation of live cattle into Israel, so the Temple Institute imported frozen embryos of red Angus cows from the United States and implanted them into the wombs of Israeli domestic cows.[4]

A few other potential candidates arose in 2018 and 2019 but also ended up being disqualified. Watching all of these cows become disqualified left some people skeptical of the entire search process. I often hear people say the search for the red heifer is being overblown and nothing will ever come of it because God is against it. Personally I have no skin in the game, and I am not a prophet, so I do not know exactly how it will play out. But what I do know is that the modern rabbinic consensus indicates this search is not going away. In fact, we see it increasing as rabbis have become officially convinced that the red heifer does not need to be born in Israel. They would prefer that it was, for sure, but they are currently getting the best results from ranches in the US.

THE FIVE RED HEIFERS FROM TEXAS (ARRIVED IN ISRAEL ON SEPTEMBER 15, 2022)

As I mentioned earlier, Clyde Lott was the first American rancher who became directly involved with the rabbis in the search for a red heifer. This set the precedent for cooperation between people in Israel and the US.

Those who have kept up with the search over the last thirty-plus years have watched with nervous optimism and toned-down expectations because only one red heifer was being examined at a time. Anticipation would rise when a heifer became a potential candidate, but disappointment followed each time a candidate was disqualified. It often took years before another candidate was singled out. This latest situation has brought about a greater level of optimism because five candidates came together at one time.

The main person behind this latest breeding effort is Byron Stinson, whom I mentioned earlier in the book. He is a businessman and part-time rancher who lives in Texas and also lives near Bethlehem during portions of the year. He loves Israel and has become a vocal member of Boneh Israel. (See chapter 5 for more information on this organization.) He has participated in many other projects in Israel that you can find on Boneh Israel's website, bonehisrael.com. Byron is known as a Gentile who shows love to the people and land of Israel by sponsoring and actively participating in these various projects.

I interviewed Byron, and you can watch our conversation on the Prophecy Watchers YouTube channel by searching for "prophecy watchers red heifer" or visiting tinyurl.com/red-heifer.

Ty Davenport and His Triple Creek Ranch

Before I go into detail about Byron's participation in the red heifer search, let's go back to 1991 and discuss Ty Davenport, whom I mentioned in chapter 5. Ty is a cattle rancher who rededicated his life to Jesus in 1991. After reading Numbers chapter 19, Ty felt the Lord revealing to him that his one purpose in life was to help fulfill prophecy and provide Israel with a red heifer.

Ty decided to change his cattle herds to Red Angus. His dad helped him find a premier Red Angus in Montana and brought it back to his ranch in Texas. These efforts took place behind the scenes, however, and Ty still did not have the personal connections he needed to help him fulfill what he perceived as his calling.

In early 2021, Jewish rabbis reached out to Byron Stinson. Byron had become friends with many of them through his connections in Israel and his work with Boneh Israel. They knew he was from Texas and had many connections with ranchers, so they asked him to help them find a red heifer. Byron's team did some research and gathered data on ranchers focused on red cattle. To improve their chances of success, they also mailed out letters, took out magazine ads, and sent text messages.

Finally, in June of 2021, they received a few responses and began to set up potential opportunities. Byron mentioned that calves are usually born in the spring or fall, and since this was June, they would have the opportunity to see the spring cattle. However, one problem surfaced: Any calves they inspected in June would have been born a month or two earlier and would have received the normal tag pierced through the ear. This tag would blemish the calf, no matter how perfectly red it was. They realized they needed to find a cow about to give birth so the new calf would not be tagged and blemished.

ROBERT MAWIRE AND GOD'S ANSWER TO PRAYER

Through providential circumstances, a gentleman from Denton, Texas, contacted me in September of 2022. He was a fan of the author L. A. Marzulli, who was filming with us in Oklahoma City at the time. The man was in possession of some giant skeletons and wanted to give them to LA, so I invited him to bring them and meet with LA. He came in October, and we had a great time of fellowship. Later, as I walked him to his car, by happenstance (cf. Ruth 2:3) I mentioned that I was working on a book about the red heifers that had just arrived in Israel on September 15.

Excitedly the man told me he was friends with a gentleman named Robert Mawire who was involved in the transaction, and said he would connect me with him. (I introduced Robert Mawire at the end of chapter 6). Mawire's office is near Fort Worth, Texas, and I had planned to be in Dallas in early December 2022 for the pre-trib.org conference. So, we set up a meeting.

Mawire is a very busy man, yet he told me he felt led by the Lord to make time for our meeting. I am extremely grateful for his graciousness and hospitality. He spent four hours with me, discussing the details of the red heifers and how he was involved. It was a true honor to gain access to firsthand information about the process.

Mawire is well known in Israel and has thirty-five years of

experience working with the Israeli government and the development of the advanced technological city of Ariel, Israel. He mentioned that a few rabbis had reached out to him, soliciting his help to procure red heifers from Texas. He is quite passionate and energetic in describing how he has learned through the years that he cannot get ahead of the Lord's guidance. So, instead of trying to do it in his own strength, he decided he would pray and wait on the Lord.

The very next day, Mawire received a phone call from his friend Brian Davenport. He did not reveal how Brian even knew to call him, but he took it as a divine answer to prayer. Brian told Mawire that his brother Ty had been raising red heifers since the 1980s. Mawire arranged a trip to meet with Ty the next day. He called Byron Stinson, and together they went to see the calves that had been born October 5–12, 2021.

Rabbis from Israel Come to Texas

A few months later, in January 2022, rabbis Chanan Kupietzky and Tzachi Mamo visited Ty Davenport's ranch in Rockwall, Texas, to observe the young red heifers. Kupietzky had been involved with Byron in other searches around the US. In March 2022, other rabbis came and inspected the cattle at the Davenport ranch. In all their searching, they found at least twenty-one cows that were potential candidates, but only five were chosen to be flown to Israel. There are still sixteen prequalified cows—and possibly more—at the ranch in Rockwall, Texas.

Israel has a restriction against importing cows into their country, so getting the heifers into the country was a challenge. Eventually, they had to label them as pets. The five cows—three of which were of the Red Angus breed and two were Santa Gertrudis—were driven from Texas to JFK airport destined for an American Airlines 777 airliner.[5]

A few more complications arose, including a requirement that the cows be insured for their flight. Byron told me this created some challenges, and the case was sent to actuaries to determine the cost of insuring the animals. The final cost for insuring the cows? Fifteen shekels per cow! In today's exchange rates, that's about

$4.03. The second challenge was that when the cows landed in Tel Aviv, the temperature had to be less than 88 degrees Fahrenheit. The mission had to be aborted twice, but the five cows finally made it to Tel Aviv on September 15, 2022.

The *Jerusalem Post* reported, "The heifers were greeted by a ceremony at Ben-Gurion Airport. Temple Institute officials Rabbi Tzachi Mamo, Rabbi Yisrael Ariel and Rabbi Azaria Ariel participated in the ceremony, alongside Stinson and Jerusalem and Heritage Ministry director-general Netanel Isaac."[6]

The cows were purchased for $100,000 each, and it cost around $200,000 to fly them to Israel.[7] Even at this significant expense, the Temple Institute and others are serious about seeing the red heifer commandment fulfilled. The cows were first taken to a secure and undisclosed location in the north, then in late 2022 and 2023 they were brought to a new location at Shiloh, the first capital of Israel, where the tabernacle stood for 369 years. The Temple Institute was in the process of building a modern visitor center where people from all over the world could come and observe the five red heifers.[8]

The Daily Wire published a nicely written article about the modern red heifer search titled "The Truth About the Red Cows in Israel." The article, written by Kassy Akiva, lists the names of the five red heifers: Segula (Protection), Geula (Redemption), Tikva (Hope), Nechama (Comfort), and Techiya (Rebirth).[9] If you visit the *Daily Wire* YouTube channel, you will find a video dated August 8, 2024, titled "Why Texan Red Heifers Were Brought to Israel—And Why It Makes Hamas So Mad," showing the five cows at Shiloh.[10]

Moriyah Shapira is the chief content officer of Ancient Shiloh, and her role includes educating visitors about the five red heifers. When asked about the timing of a future red heifer ceremony, she said, "There are no specific plans when to make the ceremony of the red heifers. That is something very important, so it needs to be agreed on first of all, among rabbis and Israelis, the people of Israel, and then among the nations. We want it to be agreeable and in a peaceful way so it will bring a blessing to the world."[11]

Yitzchak Reuven, director of international development at the Temple Institute, reported, "There is no plan right now for using a kosher red heifer, killing it and turning it into ashes. Anyone saying this is making it up. We will only do this when the time is right, because there is no point in doing it if the Jewish and rabbinic world won't accept it."[12]

These recent comments are quite different from what Byron Stinson told me when I interviewed him in the summer and fall of 2023. He told me that efforts to secure permits and permission from the Israeli government to move forward with the red heifer ceremony were already underway. He discussed the goal of performing the ceremony around Passover 2024 (April 22), and if this didn't work, then hopefully by the Jewish feast of Shavuot (June 12) later that same year. He even shared that he was working on efforts to livestream the ceremony to 800 million people. Yes, 800 million!

HAMAS ATTACK DISRUPTS THE RED HEIFER CEREMONY PLANS

In the midst of the excitement over the red heifers, something tragic and completely unexpected happened that threw a wrench in the planning of the ceremony. That tragedy occurred on October 7, 2023, the single deadliest day for Jews since the Holocaust. On that day at least 6,000 Hamas operatives and Palestinian civilians coordinated an invasion from the Gaza Strip into the Gaza Envelope of southern Israel on the Jewish religious holiday of Simchat Torah. They launched at least 4,300 rockets, flew in on powered paragliders, and broke through the border wall, attacking military bases and massacring civilians in twenty-one communities.[13] They murdered more than 1,200 men, women, and children, many of whom were kidnapped, tortured, and raped.[14] About 250 Israeli civilians and soldiers were taken as hostages to the Gaza Strip, including about 30 children.[15]

Israel immediately declared war on Hamas and has been waging war ever since to the time of this writing. No doubt this event will go down in history as adjusting the governmental focus of the Israeli Knesset. In the months leading up to the attack, there had been riots and disunity throughout the land of Israel. This all changed on October 7. After this massacre, the Israeli people realized their lives would forever be threatened by Hamas and Hezbollah unless they completely eradicated these terrorist organizations.

The Israeli operations began in the Gaza Strip in the fall of 2023, and initially Boneh Israel's plans to move forward with gaining the permits necessary to perform the red heifer ceremony on the Mount of Olives in the spring of 2024 were not affected. However, this all changed in January of 2024 when Hamas made a public statement blaming their October 7 murder spree on Israel's bringing the five red cows to Israel, claiming by doing so they had threatened the Al-Aqsa Mosque. The following is a quote from Hamas military spokesman Abu Obeida:

> We look back 100 days to remember the educated, the complicit, and the incapacitated among the world powers governed by the law of the jungle, reminding them of an aggression that reached its peak against our path (Al-Quds) and Al-Aqsa, with the start of its actual temporal and spatial division, and the *"bringing of red cows"* as an application of a detestable religious myth designed for aggression against the feelings of an entire nation in the heart of its Arab identity, and the path of its prophet (the Night Journey) and Ascension to heaven.[16]

As world leaders and journalists responded to Hamas' claims, many began to echo these words in an effort to shift the blame for the October 7 attack back on Israel. Jordanian reporter Osama Ali wrote:

> The implications of these developments extend beyond religious beliefs, delving into the political realm. The Israeli government, despite its professed secular stance, has exhibited a noteworthy eagerness to facilitate the entry and utilization of these red heifers, marking an extraordinary departure from standard procedures. This commitment, evident in both right-wing and left-wing governments, underscores the influence of religious considerations on state policies.[17]

The Red Heifer Ceremony Date Is Unknown but Anticipated

Because of comments like this from Hamas and other Muslim groups, world governments began to mount pressure against the Israeli government to seek calm in the region and avoid any unnecessary provocations by either side. The Biden administration brought especially acute pressure by withholding weapons shipments which Israel had already purchased and had legal rights to obtain. The withholding of weapons continued to some degree until the end of Biden's term.[18]

The actions by Hamas and the response by the Biden administration caused the Israeli government to be in a sticky situation in early 2024. They needed to avoid any potential conflict with the Biden administration and thus decided to forbid moving forward with the red heifer ceremony as planned for the window between Passover and Shavuot 2024 (April 22–June 12). Since early 2024 the public position by those from the Temple Institute is that the ceremony is on permanent hold.

Thoughts naturally arise as to what will be the implications of the second Trump administration and how will it affect the timing of the red heifer ceremony. No one but God knows for sure, but let me offer a few thoughts based on what we have seen in the past.

Many of you might remember that Trump was a strong supporter of Israel in his first administration, and, as mentioned earlier, he moved the embassy to Jerusalem on May 14, 2018 (modern Israel's seventieth birthday). His unwavering support for Israel caused the Mikdash Educational Center to mint a Trump/Cyrus coin in early 2018. It had a picture of Donald Trump alongside the famous Persian king Cyrus, who instructed the Jews to return to Jerusalem and build their temple after being exiled in Babylon for seventy years. In Isaiah 45:1, Cyrus is unusually called God's "messiah" (anointed one). Many of the rabbinic Jews see Trump as a non-Jewish messiah-type figure. His second administration, along with very pro-Jewish cabinet and staff, has brought new hope to all of Israel in general (for security reasons) and to the religious Jews in particular.

We are living in the age of temple preparations, red heifers being qualified, and the status quo of the Temple Mount being challenged by the national security minister, Itamar ben Gvir. Recently, there was a priestly blessing (Num. 6:21-27) done on the Temple Mount with the approval of the Israeli police. This was unprecedented and is continuing to embolden the religious Jews to seek changes in the administration of the Temple Mount.

On a side note, Saudi Arabia is rumored to desire to administer the Temple Mount instead of the country of Jordan. They give lip service to the Palestinian cause but behind the scenes do not care that much (as their actions have shown). Prior to October 7, 2024, Israel and Saudi Arabia were in serious talks of normalization. Trump also has declared his desire to bring Saudi Arabia to the table and make them part of the Abrahamic Accords.

Trump's resolute support for Israel's security and his friendship with Netanyahu has caused the religious groups to once again seek to move forward in a sense of urgency with the plans to complete the red heifer ceremony. As we saw in 2024, the Passover to Shavuot window was chosen because of the desire to coincide the ceremony with a major Jewish festival. It does not need to be in this window, but it is a convenient and joyous time of the year. The 2025 Passover to Shavuot window is April 12–June 2. As we have been saying in this book, all preparations for the temple are ready. The last piece of the third temple puzzle is the red heifer ceremony. Exciting times!

In the next chapter we will discuss the theological significance of the red heifer and the ministry of Jesus as found in the New Testament.

Chapter 9

THE NEW TESTAMENT SIGNIFICANCE OF THE RED HEIFER

FOR THE NEW Testament (New Covenant) Christian, it can be tremendously confusing to try to connect the Old Testament and New Testament. This chapter is more theological than the rest, but we need good foundational understanding. I hope that by the end of this chapter you will see how God prepared the way in the Old Testament for the coming of Jesus, and how Jesus' once-and-for-all sacrifice on the cross in the New Testament was the perfect fulfillment of the Old Covenant, securing our salvation. When you understand this, you will see why the religious Jews today who reject Jesus and the New Testament are living in a state of confusion.

THE SPIRITUAL STATE OF MOST JEWISH PEOPLE IN THE NEW TESTAMENT

Paul was a Pharisee and certainly entrenched in all things Jewish and Hebrew. He writes about his own heritage:

> If anyone else thinks he has reason for confidence in the flesh, I have more: circumcised on the eighth day, of the people of Israel, of the tribe of Benjamin, a Hebrew of Hebrews; as to the law, a Pharisee; as to zeal, a persecutor of the church; as to righteousness under the law, blameless. But whatever gain I had, I counted as loss for the sake of Christ. Indeed, I count everything as loss because of the surpassing worth of knowing Christ Jesus my Lord. For his sake I have suffered the loss of all things and count them as rubbish,

in order that I may gain Christ and be found in him, *not having a righteousness of my own that comes from the law, but that which comes through faith in Christ, the righteousness from God that depends on faith.*
—PHILIPPIANS 3:4–9, EMPHASIS ADDED

Paul understood not only the Old Testament but also the second temple literature and Jewish traditions that later became known as the rabbinic traditions. Yet he recognized that many Jews of his day sought to attain a righteousness that comes from the law and sacrifices, not from faith—and we still see this today.

Paul also wrote, "I am a Jew, born in Tarsus in Cilicia, but brought up in this city, educated at the feet of Gamaliel according to the strict manner of the law of our fathers, being zealous for God as all of you are this day" (Acts 22:3). Seeking to understand the Old Testament is not simply a matter of a difference of opinion; it is a matter of salvation. The Bible says clearly that those who reject Jesus and His salvation are not saved. There is no other way to get to the Father except through Jesus (John 14:6; Acts 4:12).

Does this mean those religious Jews today who pray many times a day, read the Old Testament, and wish to see the slaughter of the red heifer and rebuilding of the third temple take place are unsaved? This is not merely my opinion or any earthly human's, but Jesus Himself said this is the case in John 14:6: "I am the way, the truth, and the life. No one comes to the Father except through me."

Paul also writes about those Jews who do not embrace Jesus:

> Brothers, my heart's desire and prayer to God for them is that *they may be saved.* For I bear them witness that they have a zeal for God, but not according to knowledge. For, being ignorant of the righteousness of God, and seeking to establish their own, they did not submit to God's righteousness. For [Messiah] is the end of the law for righteousness to everyone who believes.
> —ROMANS 10:1–4, EMPHASIS ADDED

Paul is saying that because they were seeking to establish their own righteousness and would not submit to the righteousness that is imputed to everyone through faith in Jesus the Messiah, the Jews who did not embrace Jesus were lost and not saved.

It is not my intention to sound mean or arrogant by saying that religious Jews are confused. Paul wrote that they indeed have a zeal for God but it is not based on New Covenant knowledge (Rom. 10:3–4). They remain confused and lost because they will not embrace Jesus as Messiah. Paul writes:

> But their minds were hardened. For to this day, when they read the old covenant, that same veil remains unlifted, because only through [Messiah] is it taken away. Yes, to this day whenever Moses is read a veil lies over their hearts. But when one turns to the Lord, the veil is removed.
> —2 Corinthians 3:14-16

Paul loved his fellow Jews and sought to win them to Jesus on every occasion. He loved them and treated them with respect. I will discuss this more in a subsequent chapter. Paul was heartbroken over their refusal to seek Jesus, and we should be also (Rom. 9:1–2).

The Purpose of the Old Covenant

What, then, was the purpose of the Mosaic Law and its 613 commandments (including the red heifer commandment)? In short, these rituals, ceremonies, and commandments were given as object lessons to increase people's faith and to point forward to the time when Jesus would come and fulfill all these types and shadows. People had always been saved by grace through faith since the beginning of time.[1]

Paul discussed the value of the festivals, rituals, and holy days found under the Mosaic Law, writing:

> And you, who were dead in your trespasses and the uncircumcision of your flesh, God made alive together with him, having forgiven us all our trespasses, by canceling the record

of debt that stood against us with its legal demands. This he set aside, nailing it to the cross. He disarmed the rulers and authorities and put them to open shame, by triumphing over them in him. Therefore let no one pass judgment on you in questions of food and drink, or with regard to a festival or a new moon or a Sabbath. *These are a shadow of the things to come, but the substance belongs to [Messiah].*
—COLOSSIANS 2:13–17, EMPHASIS ADDED

Paul shows us that these rituals are simply shadows of things to come. This means they are not the real thing but instead point to a coming fulfillment, which we know is Jesus and His work on the cross. This is also true of the red heifer slaughter as found in Numbers 19.

When we come to the New Testament, this truth is not lost on the writer of the Book of Hebrews. The author of Hebrews is known to be especially skilled in Old Testament biblical theology. His goal in writing the book was to convince a group of Jews who had made a profession of faith in Jesus not to retreat back into Judaism. They were being persecuted and were contemplating forsaking their outward association with other New Covenant believers (Heb. 10:25, 34).

JESUS' SUPERIORITY OVER THE MOSAIC SYSTEM

The writer of Hebrews sought to show that Jesus was superior to the three main pillars found in Judaism: the revelation from God that came through *angels*, *Moses*, and the *Levitical priesthood*. It is written that the Old Covenant Law and understanding of the sacrificial system was given through angels, though we do not know in what capacity (Gal. 3:19; Acts 7:53). This gives the Law a tremendous level of authority, as does the fact that it was given through the prophet Moses.

Today, just as in the time of Jesus, for the Jew there is no greater prophet than Moses, who spoke with God face to face (Exod. 33:11; Num. 12:8; Deut. 34:10). Since Moses commanded that Aaron become the high priest and institute the entire Levitical system, these sacrificial ceremonies and rituals became the main focus of all Israelite worship after Moses. These practices began in the tabernacle and were followed in the temple of Solomon and all the way to the second temple of Jesus' day.

Jesus came on the scene preaching a gospel of repentance (Matt. 4:17; Mark 1:14-15) and for the purpose of offering up His life to fulfill all the requirements of the Law (Matt. 3:15; 5:17). His death would be the fulfillment of Isaiah 53, as He gave His life as a substitute for the people so that all who trusted in Him would be saved and find refuge (Ps. 2:12; Luke 24:44-48).

Many years ago, a Jewish woman began visiting the church I attended at the time. After a period of time, I realized she did not trust the Bible as being true. She told me that she did not believe in a "slaughterhouse religion" and that the idea of the blood of Jesus was not necessary. I told her I was shocked that she, as a Jewish person, could say such a thing. God instituted this "slaughterhouse religion" as centered in the tabernacle and temple precincts, with an altar on which thousands—if not millions—of animals were slaughtered over a period of 1,500 years or more (1446 BC to AD 70).

I reminded her there is consistency between Leviticus 17:11, which reads, "For the life of the flesh is in the blood, and I have given it for you on the altar to make atonement for your souls, for it is the blood that makes atonement by the life," and a similar phrase in Hebrews 9:22, which reads, "Without the shedding of blood there is no forgiveness of sins."

The Book of Hebrews begins, "Long ago, at many times and in many ways, God spoke to our fathers by the prophets, but in these last days he has spoken to us by his Son, whom he appointed the heir of all things, through whom also he created the world" (Heb. 1:1-2). The writer of Hebrews then proceeds to show that Jesus, as the Son of God, is superior to angels (Heb. 1-2). After establishing Jesus' authority, the book then focuses on the second pillar of authority: Moses.

> For Jesus has been counted worthy of more glory than Moses—as much more glory as the builder of a house has more honor than the house itself. (For every house is built by

someone, but the builder of all things is God.) Now Moses was faithful in all God's house as a servant, to testify to the things that were to be spoken later, but Christ is faithful over God's house as a son. And we are his house, if indeed we hold fast our confidence and our boasting in our hope.
—HEBREWS 3:3–6

This recognition has to be tough for a Jewish person—not only back in Jesus' day, but also today. Moses is the primary prophet a modern Jewish person looks to as the final authority. Yet Jesus is far superior and said that Moses wrote about Him (John 5:46).

Our discussion finally brings us to the third authority, which also applies to our discussion of the red heifer and the authority of the Levitical priesthood with its sacrifices. We might wonder why religious Jews are so fixated on the need to rebuild the temple and start the practice of sacrifices again. This has been their focus for the last 1,950-plus years since they rejected Jesus and the second temple was destroyed in AD 70.

We must also remember that church history has been quite shameful, considering the way many so-called Christians have treated Jewish people. These Christians slandered, persecuted, and often participated in the killing of Jewish people. This horrendous treatment was quite evident in the various expulsions, pogroms, and crusades. In fact, many Jewish people consider Hitler to be a "Christian." It is regrettable that so many Jews today would never consider following Jesus because of the actions of those who claimed to follow Him.

Granted, the inexcusable actions of some so-called Christians do not excuse the Jews for rejecting Jesus, but it should elicit in us a sense of compassion, understanding, and humility as we address the issue while speaking the truth in love (Eph. 4:15).

So, we know the writer of Hebrews shows us Jesus is better than angels and Moses, but what about the Levitical priesthood? First, the writer shows that Jesus is also a High Priest (Heb. 4–7), but His priesthood is superior because it preceded the Levitical priesthood. Jesus is considered a priest according to the superior order of Melchizedek, who was greater than Abraham (Heb. 7:1–10). So,

Jesus has a better priesthood than Levi. Next, the writer turns to the fact that even the sacrifices of Levi were inferior to the once-and-for-all sacrifice of Jesus.

OLD COVENANT SACRIFICES POINT TO JESUS

Once again, we see that the Old Testament sacrifices were a shadow pointing to something greater and more permanent to come.

> For since the law has but a *shadow* of the good things to come instead of the true form of these realities, it can never, by the same sacrifices that are continually offered every year, make perfect those who draw near. Otherwise, would they not have ceased to be offered, since the worshipers, having once been cleansed, would no longer have any consciousness of sins? But in these sacrifices there is a reminder of sins every year. For it is impossible for the blood of bulls and goats to take away sins.
> —HEBREWS 10:1–4, EMPHASIS ADDED

One of my favorite verses in the Bible is found in this chapter. It summarizes how the sacrifice of Jesus succeeded where the Old Testament sacrifices did not. Hebrews 10:14 reads, "For by one offering He has perfected forever those who are being sanctified" (NKJV). Wow! Our salvation is extremely secure because of the *one* offering of Jesus, an offering that never needs to be repeated.

In the previous chapter (Heb. 9), the writer focused specifically on the Day of Atonement sacrifice (Lev. 16) and the spiritual application of the red heifer slaughter as found in Numbers 19. He writes:

> For if the blood of goats and bulls, and the sprinkling of defiled persons *with the ashes of a heifer*, sanctify for the purification of the flesh, how much more will the blood of Christ, who through the eternal Spirit offered himself without blemish to God, purify our conscience from dead works to serve the living God. Therefore, he is the mediator of a new covenant, so that those who are called may receive the

promised eternal inheritance, since a death has occurred that redeems them from the transgressions committed under the first covenant.
—HEBREWS 9:13–15, EMPHASIS ADDED

As we saw in chapter 1, the red heifer was slaughtered to provide ashes that would be mixed with water in order to purify someone who had outwardly become ritually unclean. The unblemished and burned red heifer's ashes were a shadow pointing to the offering of Jesus. The blood of Jesus does not simply purify the externals of ritual impurity; it purifies our very conscience! Jesus was unblemished (Heb. 4:15), and His offering was far superior to that of the red heifer.

We know that the red heifer must be slaughtered and burned outside the camp (Num. 19:3). The author of Hebrews also brings up this requirement as a testimony to the connection that Jesus was the fulfillment of the red heifer slaughter. He writes, "For the bodies of those animals whose blood is brought into the holy places by the high priest as a sacrifice for sin are burned outside the camp. So, *Jesus also suffered outside the gate* in order to sanctify the people through his own blood. Therefore, let us go to him outside the camp and bear the reproach he endured" (Heb. 13:11–13, emphasis added).

JESUS IS THE ANSWER TO THE MYSTERY

This brings us to one aspect of the mystery of the red heifer that religious Jews today fail to understand: Jesus needs to be at the center. We saw earlier that a priest has to be clean to perform the ceremony, yet when a clean person gathers the ashes of the red heifer, they become unclean! The very ashes that make one person clean actually make the person who gathers them unclean. If we view this through the work of Jesus, it makes perfect sense.

When people come to the perfectly pure and clean Jesus, their sin is imputed to Him, and in a sense He becomes unclean (2 Cor. 5:21). Yet in our uncleanness, when we come to Him and interact with Him, His purity (cleanness) is transferred (imputed) to us, and we become clean! The mystery of the red heifer is solved because these are the shadows that point to Jesus. He is the fulfillment of all these Old Testament mysteries (Col. 2:16-17).

What then do we say about religious Jews trying to reinstitute the slaughter of the red heifer in our modern day? As New Covenant believers, we know these efforts will prove to be fruitless. They cannot and will not ever bring about true purification or forgiveness of sins. This can only happen through the completed and sufficient work of Jesus the Messiah for all people unto salvation—which Paul reminded us is "to the Jew first" (Rom. 1:16-17).

What the religious Jews' longing to reinstitute a means of ritual purification by way of the red heifer does reveal to us, however, is that God has a plan to save the Jewish people. Paul tells us that when the time arrives, near the end of the tribulation period, all remaining Jewish people will be saved through faith in Jesus as Messiah (Rom. 11:25-26; Zech. 12:10). In the meantime, God is allowing them to continue these fruitless efforts to slaughter the red heifer and rebuild the third temple so they will understand the extent to which they are spiritually lost.

The Antichrist will deceive the religious Jews into entering a covenant that allows them to sacrifice in the third temple, but he will betray them in the middle of the seventieth week and put an end to their sacrifices (Dan. 9:27). He will then attempt to destroy the Jews in a full genocide, but God will protect them for another three and a half years until they come to the place of repentance, when Jesus will rescue them at the end of the seven-year tribulation (Rev. 12:13-16; Matt. 23:37-39; Hos. 5:15).

What should our attitude be toward the red heifer movement and the rebuilding of the third temple? As you might imagine, there are many different viewpoints. I reached out to some of your favorite Bible teachers and asked what they thought, and I will share their answers with you in the next chapter.

Chapter 10

YOUR FAVORITE PROPHECY TEACHERS RESPOND TO THE RED HEIFER MOVEMENT

As we have seen in previous chapters, many Bible-believing Christians who love Jesus have participated in the movement to rebuild the third temple or have contributed to finding and supplying the red heifers. For the average Christian, this seeming contradiction raises some questions.

As we learned in the previous chapter, the Old Testament sacrifices, as well as any new ones that may be implemented, will not provide salvation or forgiveness, which only come through faith in the finished work of Jesus. Under the Old Covenant, the people had faith that their sacrifices were honoring to God—and they were, as long as they were performed with faith. God received their faith and accounted righteousness to them, as He did with Abraham (Gen. 15:3-6). We know that God accepted these sacrifices because they pointed forward to the full and sufficient sacrifice of Jesus.

Since we know the limitations of the sacrificial system (Heb. 10), we also know that the coming third temple, which is prophesied to be built, cannot and will not be honorable to God because it is not done by faith in Jesus. I will discuss this topic more in the next chapter, but for now let me address three questions:

1. Should Christians be excited about the preparations being made for the building of the third temple and the ritual slaughter of the red heifer?

2. Do you think God would approve of New Covenant Christians who are followers of Jesus financially contributing to the building of the third temple and the acquisition of a red heifer for Israel to ritually slaughter?

3. Would God providentially (or miraculously) provide circumstances (politically and so on) and materials for the rebuilding of the third temple and red heifer ritual slaughter without officially endorsing it?

I thought you might benefit from reading what many of today's prominent prophecy teachers think about these issues, so I asked them to share their wisdom with us. The following are their responses, with the teachers listed in alphabetical order according to their last names.

LEE BRAINARD OF SOOTHKEEP.INFO

1. Should Christians be excited about the preparations being made for the building of the third temple and the ritual slaughter of the red heifer?

> Yes. The preparations of the Orthodox for building and operating the temple, including the slaughter of the red heifer, are obviously setting the stage for the events of the seventieth week. It is hard to miss the connection between man's current efforts and God's plans for the temple in the seventieth week. The fact that the Orthodox are unbelieving is irrelevant. Just as the restoration of Israel to nation status came about through unbelieving men, Jews and Gentiles alike, who were often more political than spiritual in their focus, so the preparations for the temple are going forward through the hands of men who are unsaved. This is the sovereignty and providence of God in the background like we see in the Book of Esther. The king's heart is in the Lord's hands.
>
> But the question demands a follow-up question something along the lines of, "In what way and degree?" I have

seen a slew of material on social media with teachers hyperventilating about the red heifers and the nearness of the rapture. The rapture will be this fall or next year at the latest! The temple is going to be built next year! We won't be here next year! This is sensationalism at its finest. A healthy focus on the subject would regard the red heifers as one cog in the machinery of the temple preparations, and it would regard the temple preparations as one aspect of the prophetic convergence that is setting the stage for events that are going to happen after the church meets the Lord in the clouds. There is nothing in the temple preparations themselves or in the five red heifers from Texas that puts us on red alert for the nearness of the rapture and the rebuilding of the temple. Nothing says this fall or next year. Nothing demands in the next couple years.

One thing that needs to be understood is that there is no guarantee that any of the five will prove to be unblemished come their final test. Ditto for the red heifers being raised at several other locations in the Golan. I have been watching the red heifer story since the '80s when the focus was on finding the existing ashes. In the '90s the focus shifted to raising red heifers. Over and over again, speculation on red heifer candidates went into overdrive. The result was always the same. The overhyped information nosedived. The only thing that is certain when it comes to the current temple and red heifer developments is that the temple movement is dead serious about rebuilding the temple and vetting an unblemished red heifer and burning it for its ashes.

This earnestness is a subset of the fig-tree-generation prophecy—a significant development within the flow of events which began with the physical resurrection of the nation of Israel. In ancient Israel the temple and politics are closely intertwined. So it is now. There will be no rebuilding of the temple unless and until the current political climate changes. Ultimately, the tribulation temple will be sandwiched between the two main political figureheads of the last days: the Antichrist and the true Messiah. The false messiah will permit the rebuilding of the temple. God will own this temple as His temple. The Antichrist will sit in it, declare himself God, and erect an image in it, the whole effort being the abomination of desolation. Then the Lord will come to His temple.

Assuming that at least one of the five red heifers will remain unblemished, we have two years until their final examination if the Temple Institute follows the traditional rabbinical interpretation of the ancient sages and Rabbi Meir as taught in Mishna Parah 1:1. If they follow the minority position of Rabbi Eliezer (also mentioned in Mishna Parah 1:1), we have a wait of a year. The latter does seem to be their inclination. (See their Facebook post from September 19, 2022, entitled "More About Our 5 Red Heifer Candidates."[1]) Time will tell which of the two views prevails. But assuming that they test, sacrifice, and burn the red heifer in one year or two, they will still be at a political standstill for rebuilding the temple. The ashes will have to be stored, and the temple faithful will have to wait.

In the current political climate, there seems to be no possibility of the temple being built. Something big has to happen to change the status quo. Judging by history, we could be waiting for decades to see the temple rebuilt. This won't be the case. Most likely the big events that prepare the way will be the destruction of Israel's immediate enemies (Psalm 83), the destruction of the Gog and Magog juggernaut (Ezekiel 38–39), the rise of the Antichrist, and the treaty with many signatories. Presumably the latter will permit the rebuilding of the temple.

2. Do you think God would approve of New Covenant Christians who are followers of Jesus financially contributing to the building of the third temple and the acquisition of a red heifer for Israel to ritually slaughter?

Yes. In my mind, this is really the same question as "Does God approve of Christians helping forward the Zionist vision which sought and obtained the restoration of the nation of Israel?" If supporting Israel in general is OK, then supporting this particular aspect of Israel is OK. I would also note that God is going to own the temple as "the temple of

God" and "the holy place" during the seventieth week. This is clear in Revelation 11:1–2.

The Lord is looking forward to restoring the people and nation of Israel as His people during the seventieth week and offering them all their Old Testament promises through faith in their Messiah. This means that He was deeply involved providentially with the restoration of Israel as a nation, that He is deeply involved right now with preserving Israel for His purposes, and that He is deeply involved with the temple and red heifer projects in the background, ensuring that everything will be in place when the church is removed and the Lord returns to the people and nation of Israel. Now, if God is interested in Israel, her defense, her temple, and her post-rapture status, then I think believers ought to show an interest in these things too. Israel may be the enemy of God because of the gospel, but she is beloved of God because of His election. Perhaps this "yes" should be qualified. Our primary giving to Israel should be focused on evangelism, showing them that they do not reject Judaism when they believe on the Messiah but rather become a fulfilled Jew.

3. Would God providentially provide for the rebuilding of the temple and the procurement of the ashes of the red heifer?

Yes. As mentioned in the above paragraphs, God is working behind the scenes to have all the pieces in place when He removes the church as His earthly testimony and returns to Israel as His earthly testimony. While still in the sixty-ninth week and ostensibly working with Israel as His people and with His disciples as a saved remnant, He was working to have all the pieces in place to bring the church into existence. When the time came at the cross to tear the veil in the temple, His disciples were ready for the inauguration of the church, which occurred at Pentecost. In a similar way, the pieces are being put together now during the church age for a return to Israel for the final week of the seventy weeks. During the earthly dispensation of the sixty-ninth week, the spiritual preparations for the church age went largely unnoticed. But during the heavenly dispensation of the church age, the preparations for the seventieth week and its earthly dispensation are almost impossible to miss, at least for those with discernment.

PETE GARCIA OF REV310.NET

1. Should Christians be excited about the preparations being made for the building of the third temple and the ritual slaughter of the red heifer?

> I believe that Christians should not be overly fixated on any single third temple activity, but rather on the convergence of all these activities coming together in our day. As the old saying goes, Israel is God's prophetic timepiece. If that is true (and I believe it is), then the nation of Israel is God's hour hand, Jerusalem is God's minute hand, and the Temple Mount is God's second hand. The fact that we are seeing Israelis increasingly turning their attention to the building of a third temple, while simultaneously, Saudi Arabia and other major Islamic players are losing interest in the Temple Mount is a huge shift in the theological-geopolitical landscape. Furthermore, we are seeing the proposed train system gaining traction within Israel to connect the Ben Gurion airport in Tel Aviv to the Temple Mount in Jerusalem, which is equally amazing. Now, five "perfect" red heifers arriving in Israel, which we still have to wait and see, are simply signs upon signs that the seventieth week of Daniel is about to begin, which means our redemption draws even closer.

2. Do you think God would approve of New Covenant Christians who are followers of Jesus financially contributing to the building of the third temple and the acquisition of a red heifer for Israel to ritually slaughter?

> I don't propose to know the mind of God on these matters, but I can't see how God approves of anything that directs people's attention (or focus of affection) away from His Son, Christ Jesus, in this dispensation. However, God has

used people in the past (ex. Lord Balfour, President Truman, President Nixon, President Trump, and so on) to continue moving the prophetic ball forward according to His timeline. I suppose it will all come down to whether or not these perhaps well-intentioned Christians were doing what God called them to do, or if they were trying to "help" Bible prophecy along of their own accord.

3. Would God providentially provide for the rebuilding of the temple and the procurement of the ashes of the red heifer?

No, because an omniscient God cannot do anything without His own consent. Nevertheless, according to numerous passages in the Bible (Dan. 9:27; Matt. 24:15; 2 Thess. 2:7-8; Rev. 11), we know a third Jewish temple is going to be rebuilt. Now, whether the Jews are rebuilding this because they think their messiah has arrived (for example, Rav Shlomo Yehuda Be'eri) or because of the arrival of the Two Witnesses is anyone's guess here in the present. We just know it is going to be rebuilt, but we are not certain as to why they decided to do it. However, the prophetic conditions seem to indicate a "clearing of the plate" so to speak on the Temple Mount with the events of Ezekiel 38-39. The potential destruction of its current tenants (i.e., the Dome of the Rock and the Al-Aqsa Mosque) seems to make rebuilding the temple in their absence an irresistible situation that the Antichrist will one day desecrate, thus fulfilling the prophetic word.

DEREK P. GILBERT OF THE GILBERT HOUSE YOUTUBE CHANNEL, AND HOST OF *FIVE IN TEN* ON SKYWATCHTV

1. Should Christians be excited about the preparations being made for the building of the third temple and the ritual slaughter of the red heifer?

The excitement Christians should feel about the preparations for the third temple, including the recent revelation that several candidates for the red heifer required for the ritual purification of the kohanim who will serve in the third temple, is the anticipation of Christ's imminent return. These preparations are simply indicators that the time until His return is short.

2. Do you think God would approve of New Covenant Christians who are followers of Jesus financially contributing to the building of the third temple and the acquisition of a red heifer for Israel to ritually slaughter?

I honestly hadn't given thought to this question before now. The Temple Institute certainly directs much of its marketing to well-meaning Christians in the West. We are told by friends in Israel that American and Chinese Christians are a major source of income for the Institute.

I think it comes down to what is in one's heart. If contributions are made out of a love for Israel and the Jewish people, without a clear understanding that building the temple is not required for Christ's return, or that building the temple would lead to the reinstitution of the sacrifices described in the Law, then God will probably be forgiving. However, it's clear from Scripture that we Christians should understand that Jesus' sacrifice was the one to end all sacrifices. We don't need to shed any more blood. And, though this may surprise many Christians, our friends who live in Israel tell us most Israelis don't want a third temple! They believe that system ended when the Romans destroyed Herod's temple in AD 70. The synagogue is where religious Jews worship today, so a temple is no longer needed—besides the fact that building the third temple on the Temple Mount would trigger a regional war, if not World War III.

In fact, some Israelis consider the Temple Institute a fundraising scheme to finance the political goals of the haredim (ultra-Orthodox Jews).

3. Would God providentially provide for the rebuilding of the temple and the procurement of the ashes of the red heifer?

> It's possible that conditions for building the third temple might suddenly appear. God may allow it, to borrow a phrase from my wife, as a test and a trap. It's my view that Jewish eschatology may lead some to welcome the wrong character as Mashiach, and anyone who facilitates the building of a new temple on Mount Moriah would be identified by many as that man.

J. B. HIXSON, PHD, FOUNDER AND PRESIDENT OF NOT BY WORKS MINISTRIES (NOTBYWORKS.ORG)

1. Should Christians be excited about the preparations being made for the building of the third temple and the ritual slaughter of the red heifer?

> Yes, I think most definitely. It is a sign of the times that could very well indicate the soon coming of Christ.

2. Do you think God would approve of New Covenant Christians who are followers of Jesus financially contributing to the building of the third temple and the acquisition of a red heifer for Israel to ritually slaughter?

> I think there are two ways to look at this. Prophetically speaking, I do not think it has any bearing. We cannot hasten the return of the Lord. In terms of wisdom, does it make sense for Christians to be supporting rituals in unbelieving Israel? Probably not. But I do not see this as a moral issue. We love Israel, and we know God has a future for national Israel. So as long as a believer feels he or she is helping to lay the groundwork for true Jewish worship in the future (i.e., during the first half of the tribulation), there is probably no harm in it. But I personally would not do it because it does not seem wise to me to invest in unbelieving Israel.

3. Would God providentially provide for the rebuilding of the temple and the procurement of the ashes of the red heifer?

> Well, of course, God can "providentially" do anything. That's kind of the meaning of the term. Throughout history God has used pagan enterprises to accomplish His purposes. He used Israel's enemies, for example, to discipline His people. So, I see no problem with God orchestrating the rebuilding of the temple in unbelieving Israel without officially endorsing their worldview.

TOM HUGHES OF THE *HOPE FOR OUR TIMES* BROADCAST

1. Should Christians be excited about the preparations being made for the building of the third temple and the ritual slaughter of the red heifer?

> I would say yes and no. The yes is because we know that there's going to be a temple that's going to be built and we understand the ceremonies are going to take place again. There's going to be sacrifices and offerings. We get that. So, when we look at it from that perspective, a temple being built, red heifers, it's exciting because it's a sign that Jesus is coming again.
>
> However, the problem is that we also look at it and realize the coming temple is something that the Antichrist is going to sit in. He's going to be there demanding to be worshiped as God. He's also going to turn his persecution toward the Jews at that time. So, it's a heartbreaking thing when at the same time I'm excited about Jesus coming back. However, I'm very concerned about the Jews, the nation of Israel, and the deception that is also involved in the coming temple.

2. Do you think God would approve of New Covenant Christians who are followers of Jesus financially contributing to the building of the third temple and the acquisition of a red heifer for Israel to ritually slaughter?

> I am not somebody that would engage in doing that. I had a friend I was talking with recently about that and he said, "Look at it like this." He said, "What if somebody said, 'Hey, I'm just contributing to supply the nails that are going to crucify Jesus on the cross?'" And when you think of it like that, I think that's a very good perspective of it because we understand the dynamics that are behind everything that's there.
>
> So, I would not encourage people to engage in funding something like that, although I myself have done it in the past. Since then, I don't do it anymore. I don't think it's a good use of my funds.

3. Would God providentially provide for the rebuilding of the temple and the procurement of the ashes of the red heifer?

> That's a hard question. So, I guess we can go back to 1948 and say, OK, when we look at all the different prophecies regarding the second coming of Christ, Israel's going to be a nation again. In 1967, they're going to have Jerusalem again. You fast-forward and we realize that still in the future there is a coming temple.
>
> The sacrifices will begin again. Was God part of 1948, gathering them back together? Part of 1967? Yes. He gathered them. We know from Ezekiel chapter 37, gathering in unbelief. It will eventually turn into that place of belief. We get that. But was God acting in 1948 and 1967? Yes. So, as we look at a coming temple, the red heifer's, we know it's similar.
>
> God has laid out a plan, and God is moving everything in that direction. Does He endorse it? Well, He must endorse it in the sense of His Word tells us what's going to come. So in that regard, yes. And we know all prophecy is going to be fulfilled, every part of it (Dan. 9). What happens with the

seventieth week? Well, part of the prophecy is the temple, and it is the sacrifices that will begin again. God says that He will fulfill every single one of His prophecies.

THOMAS ICE, PHD, EXECUTIVE DIRECTOR OF THE PRE-TRIB RESEARCH CENTER (PRE-TRIB.ORG)

1. Should Christians be excited about the preparations being made for the building of the third temple and the ritual slaughter of the red heifer?

Yes, I believe it is a foreshadowing or preparation for future events that will take place after the rapture in preparation for tribulation events. In 1992 Randall Price and I co-authored a book titled *Ready to Rebuild: The Imminent Plan to Rebuild the Last Days Temple* (Harvest House). In the picture section of the book, we had a photo of a qualified red heifer named Gula from an American rancher, but before her third birthday a rabbi found five gray hairs in her tail, thus disqualifying her. Now we see, as Mondo has noted, four or five qualified heifers that could become suppliers of the ashes needed to sanctify and initiate a return of temple sacrifice in a rebuilt Jewish temple. Of course, according to prophecy this is needed by the midpoint of the tribulation, which pictures a functioning rebuilt temple. The Temple Institute in Jerusalem has already prepared the over 100 items needed for Israel's third temple. Indeed, many Jews in Israel are ready to rebuild the next temple where the Dome of the Rock currently resides.

2. Do you think God would approve of New Covenant Christians who are followers of Jesus financially contributing to the building of the third temple and the acquisition of a red heifer for Israel to ritually slaughter?

The Temple Institute in Jerusalem has raised millions of dollars to facilitate the things needed for the next Jewish temple. Likely, a majority of the funds raised so far have been contributed by Gentile Christians. In our book, *Ready to Rebuild*, we argue it is best to not financially support specific efforts to fund the rebuilding of the next temple. We should pray for and encourage the rebuilding of the temple as part of the future purpose and plan of God, but it is most likely best for the Jewish people to pay for their own efforts to construct the next temple. Certainly, it is fine for Christians to aid in the provision for a red heifer as is currently being done.

3. Would God providentially provide for the rebuilding of the temple and the procurement of the ashes of the red heifer?

Certainly, it is God's will for the third temple to be rebuilt since the prophesied events of the seventieth week of Daniel cannot take place without such a temple. Plans for the next temple are under the supervision of the reestablished body of the Sanhedrin who began meeting in October 2004 after a 1,400-year absence in Tiberias, Israel. The Sanhedrin was a council of seventy-one rabbis that governed Israel under Roman rule during the time of Christ near the temple and continued to function outside of Jerusalem (primarily in Tiberias) until around AD 400. The reinstitution of the Sanhedrin is seen as a harbinger for the rebuilding of the temple and the coming of Messiah. Orthodox Jews believe that a body like the Sanhedrin is needed today to oversee the rebuilding of the temple and to identify Messiah should He appear on the scene. This reestablished group is to decide many things related to the modern situation, such as can there be the use of electricity in a rebuilt temple. (They have decided yes.) There is nothing wrong with the third temple, even though it will be defiled by the Antichrist at the midpoint of the tribulation. The second temple was also greatly defiled by Antiochus Epiphanes before the time of Christ. Even though there has been a debate among Orthodox Jewish leadership as to whether the next temple will be the one described in Ezekiel, the modern-day Sanhedrin has settled on the fact that the next temple will be modeled after the two previous ones. It appears to me that the third temple will be officially endorsed by Jewish leadership that will oversee its rebuilding.

Nathan Jones, DRS, of Lamb and Lion Ministries and ChristInProphecy.org

1. Should Christians be excited about the preparations being made for the building of the third temple and the ritual slaughter of the red heifer?

> Yes, Christians should be excited that the third temple has been so well planned and prepared for, as it points to its soon construction, which means the even sooner return of Jesus Christ. While the Bible doesn't say what conditions lead to the Jews finally being able to build the temple on the Temple Mount in place of or adjacent to the Dome of the Rock, the most likely scenario is the stunning victory of God over Islam in the Gog-Magog War of Ezekiel 38-39. A secondary possibility is that the Antichrist's peace treaty enforces the Jewish claim to building on the Temple Mount. Either way, construction seems right around the corner, and so then does the rapture and subsequent return of Jesus Christ to set up His millennial kingdom and true temple.

2. Do you think God would approve of New Covenant Christians who are followers of Jesus financially contributing to the building of the third temple and the acquisition of a red heifer for Israel to ritually slaughter?

> Not at all. The third temple and its sacrifices have been nullified by Christ's New Covenant. To contribute to the third temple is to contribute to binding people to Judaism and the sacrificial system which does not save. Christians have far better ventures to invest their money into which would benefit people toward Christ and His salvation.

3. Would God providentially provide for the rebuilding of the temple and the procurement of the ashes of the red heifer?

"For who has known the mind of the Lord?" (Rom. 11:34).

TIM MOORE OF LAMB AND LION MINISTRIES AND CHRISTINPROPHECY.ORG

1. Should Christians be excited about the preparations being made for the building of the third temple and the ritual slaughter of the red heifer?

> Christians should be excited about any fulfillment of Bible prophecy, because it demonstrates the validity of the Word of God, the power and providence of the Almighty, and the imminence of Jesus' return. I am convinced that the third temple will not actually be constructed before the church is removed from the world at the rapture and the Antichrist is revealed. He will sign a peace treaty with the Jewish people, allowing them to finally construct their temple in Jerusalem.
>
> But, just as the appearance of Christmas decorations in the fall affirms that Christmas and Thanksgiving are just around the corner, these signs foreshadow the coming of our great God and Savior, Jesus Christ. In addition, these signs prove once again that God has not washed His hands of the Jewish people. He still plans to bring a great remnant of them to salvation. The fact that Jews are still identifiable as a people group on the earth is yet another validation of the promise and providence of God.

2. Do you think God would approve of New Covenant Christians who are followers of Jesus financially contributing to the building of the third temple and the acquisition of a red heifer for Israel to ritually slaughter?

> I think God works in ways far beyond our comprehension, but that He inspires individual Christians to serve Him individually. So, there is no question that He will motivate

some to support Jewish efforts to fulfill the prophecies outlined in Scripture. That was true a century ago when Christian Zionists avidly supported the Jewish effort to return to the Promised Land and reestablish a home and a nation. Christians do not believe Israel represents a separate means of salvation apart from our Jewish Messiah, but we take seriously God's admonition to bless His chosen people.

Likewise, we do not believe that the third temple will offer forgiveness of sins through a reconstituted sacrificial system or that the red heifer in and of itself is significant. As Hebrews 10:4 recognizes, "It is impossible for the blood of bulls and goats to take away sins." But, we also know that God's prophetic Word will be fulfilled and that, in the end, the Jews will look upon the perfect Sacrifice and weep over Him like the bitter weeping over a firstborn (Zech. 12:10).

3. Would God providentially provide for the rebuilding of the temple and the procurement of the ashes of the red heifer?

Clearly, God works all things together for our good and His glory. Even the pitiful schemes of Satan are turned in ways we do not always understand. Perhaps we can gain perspective on the third temple if we consider the first two.

David was inspired to build God a temple to replace the tent where the ark of the covenant dwelled. Nathan initially affirmed that inclination, but then returned with a word from God. The Lord asked rhetorically, "Did I speak a word with any of the judges of Israel, whom I commanded to shepherd My people Israel, saying, 'Why have you not built me a house of cedar?'" (2 Sam. 7:7, repeated in 1 Chron. 17:6). His clear insinuation was that He had not demanded a temple of wood and stone, but rather hearts that were fully devoted to Him.

Samuel established this same truth when he said, "Has the LORD as much delight in burnt sacrifices as in obeying the voice of the LORD? Behold, to obey is better than sacrifice, and to heed than the fat of rams" (1 Sam. 15:22, NASB).

Still, God did honor David's desire to build for Him a temple—although He did not allow David himself to build it.

Solomon built the first temple. Later, He took offense when the exiles who returned from Babylon neglected the building of the second temple, not because He lacked for a dwelling, but because their attitude reflected hearts that were far from Him.

The second temple was eventually completed and later made larger and grander by the great builder, Herod. In terms of official endorsement, however, even Jesus did not heap praise on the structure of the temple itself or *endorse* Herod's work. Instead, He honored its intended purpose as a "house of prayer" (Matt. 21:13). Recalling the full text of Isaiah's prophecy Jesus cited, God promised that "even those [foreigners] I will bring to My holy mountain and make them joyful in My house of prayer. Their burnt offerings and their sacrifices will be acceptable on My altar; for My house will be called a house of prayer for all the peoples" (Isa. 56:7, NASB).

So, official endorsement or gracious acceptance? I think it depends entirely on the motive of the people doing the building and the sacrificing. If they seek to please and serve the Lord, then their inclination to worship God will be honored as David's was—and the Holy Spirit will draw them to believing faith in the Lord Jesus Christ. But if they think that a building or a bull will be sufficient to appease our holy God apart from the gospel, then they are as deceived as those who cried out, "The temple of the LORD, the temple of the LORD, the temple of the LORD" in Jeremiah's day (Jer. 7:4, KJV).

In the end, we know that the third temple will be built, and that a red heifer will be sacrificed. In the fullness of time, those pre-seen historic events will give way to a time of great tribulation for the Jewish people. Only when they have come to the end of themselves will they cry out, Baruch Haba B'shem Adonai: "Blessed is He Who comes in the name of the Lord!" Then Jesus Christ will return to earth in glory and power to ascend the mountain of the Lord and reign from the throne of David.

So, while I am fascinated by all the prophetic events that are swirling around us today and converging as never before, I am not fixated on any of them individually. Instead,

I am watching and waiting—and listening for "a shout, with the voice of the archangel and with the trumpet of God" (1 Thess. 4:16, NASB), knowing that soon and very soon our Blessed Hope is coming for His bride. Are you ready?

Larry Ollison, PhD, of Larry Ollison Ministries (ollison.org)

1. Should Christians be excited about the preparations being made for the building of the third temple and the ritual slaughter of the red heifer?

Third Temple Preparations

A believer should be very excited about these current events. For one, it confirms that the Word of God is true and what was prophesied is coming to pass. Secondly, it clarifies that the interpretations of these prophecies are literal and not symbolic. Third, it's a sign that Jesus' return is closer than it has ever been.

Red Heifer Ritual

Many Christians are uneducated about the temple offerings and other offerings and rituals needed for the service and preparations.

Facts

- The church age and the temple existed side by side for forty years.
- Followers of Jesus, and this includes the disciples of Jesus, daily went into the temple, even after the resurrection. They could not enter the temple unless they were *mikveh'ed* (a ritual bath designed for the Jewish rite of purification). Why would they perform this if they were all baptized in Jesus? Why would they have to be ritually purified if they were washed in the blood of

the Lamb? Yet they still did it for years, and it was not considered blasphemous by believers. Also, they were required to be sprinkled by the ashes of the red heifer to cleanse them in case they came across a dead body.

2. Do you think God would approve of New Covenant Christians who are followers of Jesus financially contributing to the building of the third temple and the acquisition of a red heifer for Israel to ritually slaughter?

Christians Financially Contributing to the Building of the Third Temple

God knew they would be scattered and return back into the land. Rebuilding the temple is part of their "return" to God. It's a sign that God has shown them favor again.

"'I will plant them in their land, and no longer shall they be pulled up from the land I have given them,' says the LORD your God" (Amos 9:15, NKJV). The Jewish people know that the Gentiles will help with this process. Even King Cyrus and Darius helped out with supplying resources for the second temple.

"Even those from afar shall come and build the temple of the LORD. Then you shall know that the LORD of hosts has sent Me to you. And this shall come to pass if you diligently obey the voice of the LORD your God" (Zech. 6:15, NKJV).

Notice in Revelation, it is John who measures the temple. It clearly states, it is the *temple of God*! Not only the temple of God is measured, but in total, three things are measured: 1) the temple *of God*; 2) the altar; and 3) those who worship there (the priest / *Cohen* / sons of Aaron) and the Levis. "Then I was given a reed like a measuring rod. And the angel stood, saying, 'Rise and measure the temple of God, the altar, and those who worship there'" (Rev. 11:1, NKJV). Two of these three things physically exist today: the altar and the priests!

John writes and clearly states that this third temple is *not* the beast's/Antichrist's temple. It's God's and only God's temple. A person can say it's theirs; Donald Trump could help build it and says it's his building. Even the Antichrist can say it's his building. However, it does not matter which man or even any angel who decides to lay claim to this structure. It's God's house, and He gives it to no one. Paul confirms this very point for the sign of the coming of the Lord: "Let no one deceive you by any means; for that Day will not come unless [1] the falling away comes first, and [2] the man of sin is revealed, the son of perdition, who opposes and exalts himself above all that is called God or that is worshiped, so that he sits as God in the temple of God, showing himself that he is God" (2 Thess. 2:3-4, NKJV).

Here we have two clear verses that this coming third temple is and always will be God's house. Just because the man of sin declares he is "God" in the third temple, does not make it the Antichrist's temple. *It will never be his house.* For a believer to declare the next temple as the Antichrist's temple is a direct, rebellious, and degrading of God's house, God's authority, and God's complete sovereign ownership. Do we not understand that this is the sole purpose of the Antichrist, to declare that God's possessions are his and that he is god?

Thus, now knowing that John and Paul, under the direction of the Holy Spirit, declared the third temple as God's temple, is it not a good thing that Christians contribute to the house of God? Especially if that very *house* resides in Israel, in Jerusalem on Mount Zion. Would it be considered *the abomination* if it were not God's house? This proves the point that the great *abomination that causes desolation* wouldn't be such a big deal unless it's done in God's land, in God's city, on God's holy mountain, *in God's house.* That is the ultimate sign of *an abomination.*

Final point: In Jesus' days on this earth, before the resurrection, the state of the Israeli government, especially the temple state, was at an all-time low. Corruption was rampant; high priests serving in the temple were not even sons of Aaron but appointed by the highest bidder and influenced by the Roman government. Yet Jesus still called it "My house"!

- I. "And He said to them, 'It is written, "My house shall be called a house of prayer," but you have made it a "den of thieves"'" (Matt. 21:13, NKJV).
- II. "Then He taught, saying to them, 'Is it not written, "My house shall be called a house of prayer for all nations"? But you have made it a "den of thieves"'" (Mark 11:17, NKJV).
- III. "Saying to them, 'It is written, "My house is a house of prayer," but you have made it a "den of thieves"'" (Luke 19:46, NKJV).

Jesus confirms 1) the complete corruption; 2) it's His house; and 3) more importantly, the entire purpose for the temple is '*a house of prayer*'!

Acquisition of the Red Heifer

Revelation 11 confirms there will be a third temple, and in order for that temple to operate, the ashes of the red heifer will have to be used. By confirming that this temple and the other temples are for a house of prayer, and it's God's house, the red heifer is needed to cleanse the land due to many years of bloodshed, cleanse the people who will enter it, and cleanse the articles needed for the service. The Book of Hebrews explains that it's the flesh that was needed of the ashes of the red heifer, and that Jesus has performed a higher cleansing that is on another level, to cleanse one's conscience (spiritually).

For if the blood of bulls and goats and the ashes of a heifer, sprinkling the unclean, sanctifies for the purifying of the flesh, how much more shall the blood of Christ, who through the eternal Spirit offered Himself without spot to God, cleanse your conscience from dead works to serve the living God?

—HEBREWS 9:13-14, NKJV

3. Would God providentially provide for the rebuilding of the temple and the procurement of the ashes of the red heifer?

> I think the answers above help clarify the endorsements of these last-day miracles. However, here are more proofs. There have only been nine red heifers since the time of Moses, until now. Jews look for the days of the tenth red heifer as a sign of the coming of the Messiah. In 2022, now there are five perfect red heifers. Only God can create such an animal, and it is considered a modern-day miracle, and God is restoring fellowship with His people once again.

BILL SALUS OF PROPHECY DEPOT MINISTRIES (WWW.PROPHECYDEPOTMINISTRIES.NET)

1. Should Christians be excited about the preparations being made for the building of the third temple and the ritual slaughter of the red heifer?

> This is a bittersweet topic. On the sweet side, Christians can point out that the third temple was prophesied to become a reality in the end times. We find references to this in several passages such as Revelation 11:1-2; Matthew 24:15; and 2 Thessalonians 2:4. As such, the coming third temple can be used to "eschatologically evangelize."
>
> On the bitter side, this coming temple, although foreknown by God, is not endorsed by Him. The reinstatement of animal sacrifices by the Jewish people as part of the antiquated Mosaic Law blatantly ignores the fact that Christ's sacrificial death upon the cross fulfilled the Law and ended the sacrificial system. (Read Matthew 5:17-18; Romans 8:3-4; and Galatians 3:23-25.)

2. Do you think God would approve of New Covenant Christians who are followers of Jesus financially contributing to the building of the third temple and the acquisition of a red heifer for Israel to ritually slaughter?

> I apologize if this next answer sounds facetious, but the third temple will be constructed with or without the financial contributions of Christians. So, why would a Christian waste their hard-earned funds on this project? There are far better ministries to tithe into. Especially since the temple's intended activities of sacrifices and offerings are futile and not endorsed by God. (Read Psalm 50:7-15.)
>
> According to Luke 22:19-20, Christ shed His blood in order to inaugurate a better New Covenant. Presently, atonement is available through Jesus Christ and not the red heifer. Save your money and invest it wisely into the kingdom of God.

3. Would God providentially provide for the rebuilding of the temple and the procurement of the ashes of the red heifer?

> One of the primary reasons the Jews want to build this temple and reinstate animal sacrifices is to hasten the coming of their Messiah. They reject Jesus Christ as the Messiah. Isaiah 28:14 appropriately accuses these Jewish leaders as "scornful men, who rule this people who are in Jerusalem" (NKJV). As such, why would God go out of His way to help these Christ-rejecting, scornful rulers?
>
> I don't see any reason that the Lord would providentially or politically sponsor this temple building effort. The reality that these scornful rulers are going to discover is that the third temple doesn't hasten the first coming of their "Messiah," which happened about two thousand years ago, but it will hasten His second coming at the end of the tribulation period!

David Schnittger, DMin, of Southwest Prophecy Ministries (www.swpm.us)

1. Should Christians be excited about the preparations being made for the building of the third temple and the ritual slaughter of the red heifer?

> I believe Christians can be "excited" about the preparations for the third temple in that it does represent a fulfillment of Bible prophecy. This would be similar to our excitement in Israel becoming a nation in 1948 in fulfillment of Bible prophecy. I do not think the intention of the Temple Faithful is to build a temple that will eventually be occupied by the son of perdition (2 Thess. 2:3-4, NKJV). It is not at all clear that this occupancy occurs with the willing participation of the Jews, as this occurs at the height of power by the Antichrist (Rev. 13). It is my understanding that the rebuilding of the third temple by the temple faithful anticipates the return of the Messiah. As Maurice Jaffe, former president of the Jerusalem Great Synagogue, said to me in April 1977, "It may be that the Messiah we anticipate and the One you worship are one and the same." We know that the spiritual blinders will be lifted for the Jewish remnant at the second coming (Zech. 12:10).

2. Do you think God would approve of New Covenant Christians who are followers of Jesus financially contributing to the building of the third temple and the acquisition of a red heifer for Israel to ritually slaughter?

> I would relegate the answer to that to the category of "disputable things" dealt with in Romans 14:10-19. I default to Romans 14:19 (KJV): "Let us therefore follow after the things which make for peace, and things wherewith one may edify another." I am fine with other Christians contributing to this project as long as they do not judge me for choosing *not* to contribute.

3. Would God providentially provide for the rebuilding of the temple and the procurement of the ashes of the red heifer?

I believe that everything that occurs is by the providential will of God, but that does not answer your question. In regard to God's providence for this particular project, I believe the sovereign hand of God will *guarantee* that every jot and tittle of His prophetic Word will be fulfilled to the letter. As to whether this constitutes the moral or "prescriptive" will of God, I have my doubts. After all, Romans 11:25 (KJV) states, "Blindness in part is happened to Israel, until the fulness of the Gentiles be come in." In my view, this reality should temper our view of, and participation in, projects by Jewish religious leaders.

It is for this reason that I think the term "Zionist Christian" should be used with qualification. In my personal view, I am reticent to add any adjectives to my status as a "Christian." I believe this term, if rightly understood, is all-encompassing.

By the way, the anticipation of the ashes of the red heifer go all the way back to the mid-1970s when I was just getting my start at Southwest Radio Church. All that to say that *patience* is required for the fulfillment of prophetic scriptures.

GARY STEARMAN OF PROPHECY WATCHERS (PROPHECYWATCHERS.COM)

1. Should Christians be excited about the preparations being made for the building of the third temple and the ritual slaughter of the red heifer?

Since 1948, and even before that, contemporary Israel has dreamed of building a new temple, one that they believe will prepare them for the coming of Messiah. Visitors to Israel make the mandatory stop at the Jerusalem Temple Institute to see what has been planned for the very near future. There is something very exciting about visualizing the moment of finality in the process of building what will one day become the world's most important edifice. But the temple needs a priesthood, and it must be ritually cleansed and dedicated before worship can take place there.

Those who are preparing for priestly service realize that they have reached the critical point in that process that requires a very special ceremony. It involves a particular setting and procedure. To them, it is a necessity (despite the dramatic effect that it would have in the world of Israel's enemies) to prepare for the cleansing of the Jewish temple and its officials. To bring about a functioning priesthood, Israel must prepare the cleansing ashes of the red heifer. Christians who study Bible prophecy and are familiar with God's instructions to Moses in Numbers chapter 19 are (and should be) extremely excited at this—the next vital step toward temple worship!

2. Do you think God would approve of New Covenant Christians who are followers of Jesus financially contributing to the building of the third temple and the acquisition of a red heifer for Israel to ritually slaughter?

At Israel's very beginning, God took Abraham, Isaac, and Jacob on a series of journeys, where they encountered Gentile tribes of every description. Some were openly hostile. Others were pretenders, whose real motive was to loot the blessings given to the twelve tribes. But many were led of the Lord to bring aid and comfort to Israel. Of course, God knew in advance about the variability of humankind, and He told Abraham what to expect. From that time to the present moment, the terms of His covenant ring out with a clarity and directness that leaves not the slightest doubt about Israel's position in the world system:

Now the LORD had said unto Abram, Get thee out of thy country, and from thy kindred, and from thy father's house, unto a land that I will shew thee: And I will make of thee a great nation, and I will bless thee, and make thy name great; and thou shalt be a blessing: And I will bless them that bless thee, and curse him that curseth thee: and in thee shall all families of the earth be blessed.

—GENESIS 12:1–3, KJV

In various ways, the Bible tells us that the third temple will be erected amidst great conflict and apostasy. But many in Israel have been blessed by Gentile assistance and funding. Bible-believing Christians know that they must bring aid and comfort to Israel where that is possible. And they also know that God will honor and approve their intentions.

3. Would God providentially provide for the rebuilding of the temple and the procurement of the ashes of the red heifer?

God's timing is perfect. And He provides for His people, as can be seen dozens of times throughout Scripture. Will God provide the necessities of building the third temple? The answer to this question is that He has already done so... many times. Individuals and organizations from all over the world have donated their time, talent, and money to Israel. Those dedicated to the future priesthood know that offerings to Israel will be directed by the Lord, and that it is His will that Gentiles bless Israel, the most important nation on the face of the earth.

In the near future, the third temple will become extremely important. They also know that several global conflicts must come to pass in the process. As regards God's contemporary dealings with Israel, we have only to look at recent history. He has certainly given them a series of magnificent blessings in their return to the Promised Land in the era following the First Zionist Congress in 1897. And key events among the Gentile world powers brought the Balfour Declaration in 1917. Then, following World War II, many Europeans aided Jews who were returning to their land. Behind the scenes, God's actions have brought political, military, and financial aid to a struggling postwar Israel. It is logical to think that He will continue in the same way.

Amir Tsarfati of Behold Israel (beholdisrael.org)

Amir did not answer my questions specifically, but the following is from a public compilation in his Telegram post on September 17, 2022, and a YouTube video addressing this topic titled "Amir Tsarfati: The True Meaning of Rosh Hashanah," posted on September 22, 2022.

> Allow me to be very honest with you and say that all things pertaining to the third temple in Jerusalem bring anything BUT excitement to me. Whether it's the blue prints of the building that are ready, the training of people for animal sacrifice, or the periodical resurfacing of red heifers to the scene—they are but one more reason for us to pray for the salvation of Israel, not to rejoice with them.
>
> The imagery of the red heifer is yet another foreshadowing of the sacrifice of Christ for believers' sins. The Lord Jesus was "without blemish," just as the red heifer was to be. As the heifer was sacrificed "outside the camp" (Numbers 19:3), Jesus was crucified outside of Jerusalem (Hebrews 13:11-12). And just as the ashes of the red heifer cleansed people from the contamination of death, so the sacrifice of Christ saves us from the penalty and corruption of death. To see the Jews rejoice in the shadow of the cow and reject the substance of Christ is sad.
>
> Instead of us trying to guess how close the rapture is, why don't we all use these events to pray for the veil to be lifted and for the substance to be recognized. Israel is about to go through the biggest deception followed by a more terrible Holocaust than ever before. All of which is sadly connected to that temple, as it will serve as the seat of a pseudo-messiah who will get his power, authority, and throne from Satan himself.
>
> Therefore, we, who know the truth and are eagerly waiting for our savior to come and take us any day now, must refrain from celebrating these sad events of a blind nation that will suffer greatly.
>
> "But their minds were blinded. For until this day the same

veil remains unlifted in the reading of the Old Testament, because the veil is taken away in Christ. But even to this day, when Moses is read, a veil lies on their heart. Nevertheless when one turns to the Lord, the veil is taken away" (2 Corinthians 3:14-16, NKJV).

The church is not to be excited about the third temple. The church is not to be excited about those things that are actually going to confuse and deceive the Jewish people to think that they do have a way to God now, even without Christ....Yes, for the Jews it's a Messianic sign. Yes, for the Jews, it is full of excitement. But for us, for us who know exactly what the third temple is going to bring about for the Jewish people...[this is] bad news. It will be terrible.[2]

ANDY WOODS, PHD, OF ANDY WOODS MINISTRIES (ANDYWOODSMINISTRIES.ORG)

1. Should Christians be excited about the preparations being made for the building of the third temple and the ritual slaughter of the red heifer?

Should we be excited about those things? I would argue yes. Not because I'm trying to reverse the Book of Hebrews and go back to animal sacrifice. That's not why I'm excited about it. I'm excited about it because those things have to be functioning for the tribulation period scenario to come into existence. And so, what I'm trying to say is, midway through the tribulation period, the Antichrist will go into the rebuilt Jewish temple and put an end to animal sacrifices.

That means by the time you get to the midpoint, there has to be a temple built and there has to be a sacrificial system implemented. So the fact that these things are starting to happen now, it shows me that the seven-year tribulation period is approaching, and the reason I'm excited about that is, I'm of the perspective that the rapture or the translation of the church takes place before the tribulation period even begins.

The signs of the tribulation period don't just tell me that the tribulation period is coming, but they tell me that the rapture is coming even faster. That's why I'm excited about it. It's like the old adage when you see the signs of Christmas, Santa Claus, Christmas tree lights, Christmas songs in the department store, you know that Thanksgiving is coming because Thanksgiving occurs earlier on the calendar than Christmas. So, yeah, that's why I'm excited about it.

2. Do you think God would approve of New Covenant Christians who are followers of Jesus financially contributing to the building of the third temple and the acquisition of a red heifer for Israel to ritually slaughter?

I would say it's a freedom in Christ issue because I don't have a verse in the Bible that says, "Thus saith the Lord, 'You shall never assist or contribute to that kind of a project.'" I mean, if a believer individually, through their own volition and conscience, feels called to be involved in that, I don't think there's any biblical prohibition against them.

However, I would say that being involved in that is not the primary purpose of the church. Jesus gave us our instructions in the Great Commission, and part of those is not to fund the red heifer and these kinds of things. So, I'm of the view that God is pretty good at fulfilling His prophecies. Whether I help Him or not, He really doesn't need my help. I don't see that as something I have to do. I don't see that as the primary calling and mission of the church collectively. But at the same time, if an individual Christian feels called to be involved in that, I don't see any prohibition against it. So, I would just look at it as kind of a freedom and Christ balance issue.

If you want to do that, I think you have the freedom to do it. Just don't put it on the whole church, universal or local, and say, you know, we all have to do this, because that's not our primary mandate.

3. Would God providentially provide for the rebuilding of the temple and the procurement of the ashes of the red heifer?

I don't think God ever endorses animal sacrifices, at least the way we're describing it, because the Book of Hebrews is very clear that Jesus is the fulfillment of the animal sacrifices. So, when He fulfills His Word, He's not doing it as an endorsement. This is what Israel in unbelief is going to do. These are the circumstances that are necessary for unbelieving Israel to one day become believing Israel.

That's how God is working. It's with the end goal of leading Israel to faith alone, in Christ alone. They've got to be knocked down before they look up. They've got to be in a situation where the Antichrist betrays them by putting an end to these things. And that's what's going to sort of shock them, if you will, into faith in the second half of the tribulation period. That's God's end product. That's His endgame. He can provide providentially for the rebuilding of these things for that purpose. But that shouldn't be misconstrued as God is applauding animal sacrifices in and of itself.

Chapter 11

SEEKING A BALANCED BIBLICAL OUTLOOK ON THE RED HEIFER MOVEMENT

IN THE PREVIOUS chapter we had the opportunity to read a variety of opinions presented by prophecy teachers whom God has raised up in these times. I love and respect these teachers and have interviewed almost all of them at one time or another. Each one of them loves Jesus and His Word, and they are all operating according to the convictions they hold after years of studying the Scripture. But did you notice that not all of them agreed perfectly on the three questions I asked? I actually believe these variations in opinions to be very positive.

My goal in this chapter is to build a foundation for understanding the role of Israel in the plan of God and how this plan will unfold in the final developments at the end of the age. I also want to address the current New Testament theological perspective on the second temple and the secular and religious Jewish people today who do not have faith in Jesus as the Messiah. This foundational understanding will help by giving us a thoroughly biblical framework for assessing the third temple developments, including the red heifer. I will tackle these topics first and then give my opinions on the three questions I asked my brothers in the previous chapter.

What Does the New Testament Teach About the Second Temple and Its Destruction?

If you have not read chapter 9 of this book in a while, I encourage you to refresh yourself with the teaching there, as it relates to Paul's heart for his unsaved Jewish brethren, and also the meaning of the red heifer as a type and shadow that pointed to the final sacrifice of Jesus. What we learn from the entire Book of Hebrews and its history is that God's work through a temple and sacrifices was finished in this age at the time of Jesus. This topic can be very complicated, so we will take it one step at a time.

Jesus told the woman at the well that a time would soon arrive when people would worship the Father not in Jerusalem but in spirit and in truth (John 4:21-24). In addition, the Bible teaches us that when Jesus died, the veil of the temple was torn in two from top to bottom. This definitive miracle performed by God was proof that Jesus had started something new, providing us access to God that did not involve a physical temple (Matt. 27:51). We read on several occasions that the institutions of the second temple continued operating for a period of time after Jesus ascended into heaven, but its influence slowly faded away into obsolescence.

Paul writes concerning the old covenant, "Indeed, in this case, what once had glory has come to have no glory at all, because of the glory that surpasses it. For if what was *being brought to an end* came with glory, much more will what is permanent have glory" (2 Cor. 3:10-11, emphasis added). Paul was contrasting the glory of the old covenant under Moses with the surpassing glory of the new covenant under the Spirit. The old covenant glory was brought to an end at Christ's death and replaced with the permanent glory of the new covenant.

The New Covenant Supersedes the Old Covenant

The author of Hebrews writes something similar about the new covenant versus the old covenant: "In speaking of a new covenant, he makes the *first one obsolete*. And what is *becoming obsolete* and growing old is *ready to vanish away*" (Heb. 8:13, emphasis added).

The second temple still stood when the Book of Hebrews was written, but the writer understood that it would soon be destroyed and that any semblance of the second temple and old covenant would be permanently removed and vanish away. That happened in AD 70 and is a testimony to the fact that God was finished with the second temple and its sacrifices because Jesus fulfilled them.

It is important to note that the second temple system was not inherently evil nor wicked but was part of the revelation of God, and God originally encouraged its reconstruction. (See Haggai 1:8 and Romans 7:12.) However, once Jesus came and fulfilled the old covenant system, it was replaced with the new covenant and a new high priesthood of Jesus through the order of Melchizedek (Heb. 7).

In fact, the author of Hebrews tells us explicitly that this old covenant Levitical system was annulled through the work of Jesus, and a physical temple was no longer required after the change to the new covenant system of law.

> Therefore, if perfection were through the Levitical priesthood (for under it the people received the law), what further need was there that another priest should rise according to the order of Melchizedek, and not be called according to the order of Aaron? *For the priesthood being changed, of necessity there is also a change of the law.* For He of whom these things are spoken belongs to another tribe, from which no man has officiated at the altar. For it is evident that our Lord arose from Judah, of which tribe Moses spoke nothing concerning priesthood. And it is yet far more evident if, in the likeness of Melchizedek, there arises another priest who has come, not according to the law of a fleshly commandment, but according to the power of an endless life. For He testifies: "You are a priest forever according to the order of Melchizedek." *For on the one hand there is an annulling of the former commandment* because of its weakness and unprofitableness, for the law made nothing perfect; on the other hand, there is the bringing in of a better hope, through which we draw near to God.
>
> —HEBREWS 7:11–19, NKJV, EMPHASIS ADDED

Under the old covenant, people were required to make sacrifices to demonstrate their faith and obedience in following the commandments of God. Once the new covenant was established at the last supper and finalized with the death and resurrection of Jesus, sacrifices were no longer required to please God (Luke 22:20). The veil was torn, and everyone was granted access to the holy of holies, not through sacrifices but through faith in Jesus.

> Therefore, brothers, since we have confidence to enter the holy places by the blood of Jesus, *by the new and living way that he opened for us through the curtain, that is, through his flesh,* and since we have a great priest over the house of God, let us draw near with a true heart in full assurance of faith, with our hearts sprinkled clean from an evil conscience and our bodies washed with pure water.
> —Hebrews 10:19–22, emphasis added

The Book of Hebrews was written primarily to Jews to show them the insufficiency of the Levitical and temple sacrifices. These sacrifices served a holy purpose under the old covenant, but now that the new covenant had been established by the once-and-forever sacrifice of Jesus, reliance on the temple sacrifices would be misplaced. The author reminds them that those sacrifices *never* truly took away sins anyway but were simply pointing to the final sacrifice that the Messiah Jesus accomplished. "For since the law has but a *shadow of the good things* to come instead of the true form of these realities, it can never, by the same sacrifices that are continually offered every year, make perfect those who draw near.... For it is *impossible* for the blood of bulls and goats to take away sins" (Heb. 10:1, 4, emphasis added).

The Transition Period from the Old Covenant into the New

We know the second temple was not destroyed until AD 70. This means a transition period occurred between the establishment of the new covenant through the offering of Jesus and the destruction and removal of the second temple four decades later.

Remember, the first believers in Jesus were Jews who had 1,500 years of sacrificial history and traditions that God knew would be hard for them to break. (See Acts 10:10-17 as one example.) Therefore, it is no surprise that most Jewish believers in Jesus maintained their traditions and visited the second temple up until it was destroyed. We read about Peter, John, and the other apostles teaching in the temple precincts (Acts 2-5), and many years later Paul went to the second temple to make some offerings and evangelize in the courts (Acts 21). Did their visits to the temple indicate they did not believe the sacrifice of Jesus was enough? Not at all.

Peter stated quite clearly that the Law of Moses and all its commandments was a heavy yoke that none of them could handle. He also stated that the Gentiles would be saved by grace just like the Jewish believers under the new covenant. Peter said, "Now, therefore, why are you putting God to the test by placing a yoke on the neck of the disciples that neither our fathers nor we have been able to bear? But we believe that we will be *saved through the grace* of the Lord Jesus, just as they will" (Acts 15:10-11, emphasis added).

God put His stamp of approval on the final sacrifice of Jesus when He tore the veil in the holy of holies. With this act God showed He would no longer need or demand future sacrifices, and any sacrifice made after this point would not be accepted as legitimate. But what about Paul and others participating in the second temple services? God did not command these sacrifices, but I believe He allowed them during this transition period, knowing the issue would soon become irrelevant because the second temple would be destroyed a few decades later.

In addition, offerings of sacrifice performed by Jewish believers during this transition period were made in connection with their faith in Jesus. They likely understood the theology of the Book of Hebrews and that the sacrifice of animals could not provide forgiveness of sin, which was only made possible by the blood of Jesus under the new covenant.

This concept is relevant to our discussion of the idea of modern religious Jews building the third temple. Will God accept their sacrifices? The Book of Hebrews would teach absolutely not. Why not? Because their offering of sacrifices was *far* different from what we saw with the first-century Jewish Christians. How so? Because Paul and the other first-century Jews made their sacrifices in tandem with faith in Jesus and His final offering, His once-and-for-all sacrifice.

Make no mistake: When the modern religious Jews offer sacrifices in the coming third temple, they will *not* be mixed with faith in the sacrifice of Jesus. This is why I believe God will not honor their sacrifices.

Non-Christian religious Jews today are not ignorant of the person of Jesus of Nazareth. Some are indifferent, but many despise and hate Him. Instead of calling Jesus by His Hebrew name, "Yeshua," many Jews today call Him "Yeshu," an acrostic dating back to early rabbinic times that means "may his name and memory be blotted out."[1] This is blasphemy and is well known in many religious circles. Sadly, even some secular people call Jesus by this name; I would hope many of them are unaware of this acrostic association.

HISTORICAL EVIDENCE FOR THE PASSING AWAY OF THE OLD COVENANT

There is one piece of rabbinical tradition that I am surprised to find included in Talmudic literature. Most New Testament scholars believe that Jesus was crucified around AD 30–33. There is some variation, but this is the general consensus. The second temple was destroyed in AD 70, which is approximately forty years after Jesus ascended into heaven.

The Talmud in Yoma 39b reads:

> Forty years before the Temple was destroyed the chosen lot was not picked with the right hand, nor did the *crimson stripe* turn white, nor did the westernmost light burn; and the doors of the Temple's Holy Place swung open by themselves, until Rabbi Yochanon ben Zakkai spoke saying: "O most Holy Place, why have you become disturbed? I know full well that your destiny will be destruction, for the prophet Zechariah ben Iddo has already spoken regarding you saying:

'Open thy doors, O Lebanon, that the fire may devour the cedars' (Zechariah 11:1)."[2]

Interestingly, the crimson stripe was a reference to a cloth tied to the scapegoat for the Day of Atonement (Lev. 16:21-22). The crimson cloth is not mentioned specifically in the biblical passage, but rabbinical tradition holds that a red cloth was tied to the goat, and another red cloth was kept in the temple precincts. When the goat was sent away and the sacrifices were completed, the red cloth would miraculously turn white as evidence that God had forgiven the people's sin and atonement was completed. Yet here the rabbinical literature clearly says that the red cloths stopped turning white about forty years before the second temple was destroyed. This is ancient evidence, in their own writings, of God miraculously showing the Jews that their sacrificial offerings of the second temple were no longer providing atonement.

Is this story 100 percent true? I have no way to verify it, but the fact that rabbis report it themselves with no explanation as to why gives it a level of authenticity, in my opinion. Also, the timing coincides exactly with the death and resurrection of Jesus as the final sacrifice and the implementation of the new covenant that we read about in the New Testament. The second temple veil was torn, a miraculous event that showed God no longer required Levitical sacrifices in order for anyone to access the holy of holies. This powerful testimony helps shape our understanding of how God will view the coming third temple sacrifices.

The Parable of the Wicked Tenants

As we conclude this section, we must remember what is at stake. God sent His beloved Son to die as a substitute for His people (Isa. 53), and instead of responding to Jesus with repentance and acceptance, the Jews plotted to kill Him.

Soon before Jesus was arrested, He told this parable:

> "Hear another parable. There was a master of a house who planted a vineyard and put a fence around it and dug a winepress in it and built a tower and leased it to tenants, and

went into another country. When the season for fruit drew near, he sent his servants to the tenants to get his fruit. And the tenants took his servants and beat one, killed another, and stoned another. Again he sent other servants, more than the first. And they did the same to them. Finally he sent his son to them, saying, *'They will respect my son.'* But when the tenants saw the son, they said to themselves, 'This is the heir. Come, let us kill him and have his inheritance.' And they took him and threw him out of the vineyard and killed him. When therefore the owner of the vineyard comes, what will he do to those tenants?" They said to him, *"He will put those wretches to a miserable death and let out the vineyard to other tenants who will give him the fruits in their seasons."* Jesus said to them, "Have you never read in the Scriptures: 'The stone that the builders rejected has become the cornerstone; this was the Lord's doing, and it is marvelous in our eyes'? Therefore, I tell you, the kingdom of God will be taken away from you and given to a people producing its fruits. And the one who falls on this stone will be broken to pieces; and when it falls on anyone, it will crush him." *When the chief priests and the Pharisees heard his parables, they perceived that he was speaking about them.* And although they were seeking to arrest him, they feared the crowds, because they held him to be a prophet.
—MATTHEW 21:33–46, EMPHASIS ADDED

We learn several things from this parable. Jesus notes that the master of the vineyard (God) sent many servants (prophets), who were killed by the tenants (Jewish leadership). Finally, the master sends his son (Jesus), believing the tenants will respect him. Instead, the tenants kill the master's son. Jesus then asked the Pharisees what they thought the master would do to the tenants for killing his heir, and they acknowledged that he would be correct to put the wretches to a miserable death and replace the leadership. Matthew tells us the chief priests and Pharisees knew this parable was speaking about them, yet instead of repenting, they wanted to arrest Jesus.

Jesus Pronounces Judgment on Jerusalem for Rejecting Him

About this same time, Jesus came into Jerusalem.

> And when he drew near and saw the city, he wept over it, saying, "Would that you, even you, had known on this day the things that make for peace! But now they are hidden from your eyes. For the days will come upon you, when your enemies will set up a barricade around you and surround you *and hem you in on every side and tear you down to the ground, you and your children within you. And they will not leave one stone upon another in you, because you did not know the time of your visitation.*"
> —LUKE 19:41–44, EMPHASIS ADDED

Jesus pronounced judgment on Jerusalem, the temple, and the people of Israel because their leadership refused to recognize the time of His prophetic and long-awaited arrival. Because they rejected Jesus, the city of Jerusalem and the temple were destroyed in AD 70, and many people were killed.

When God tore the veil of the temple in two from top to bottom, He provided miraculous evidence that the old covenant system of atonement through ceremonial sacrifice was finished and that any future sacrifices would be rejected. Jesus was the final sacrifice. Even after the crucifixion, resurrection, and ascension of Jesus, the Jewish people and their leadership refused to recognize their sin and continued to persecute His followers (Acts 3–12). Finally, after providing a forty-year window of witnessing to the people of Israel in hopes that they would accept His Son as the final sacrifice, God closed that window with the destruction of the second temple.

The Spiritual Condition of National Israel Today

I have carefully nuanced the title of this section to write about "national Israel," referring to Israel before it officially became a nation. Think of it as a corporate entity like we find in the Old Testament. Even when God sent national Israel into exile in the

Babylonian captivity as a result of their sin, faithful individuals like Daniel, Ezekiel, Jeremiah, and others also suffered for the judgment of their nation. Israel's leadership was wicked, and God often judged the nation according to its leadership. Many of us today don't understand this theological principle because of our individualistic thinking, but we do observe it in the Old Testament.

Remember when David sinned by taking a census in 2 Samuel 24? Although it was David who sinned, seventy thousand people died in a plague as the judgment for his sin (1 Chron. 21:14). David himself did not die. In the first century, similar judgment came on corporate Israel when their chief priests and leaders rejected Jesus, even calling down a curse on themselves and their children (Matt. 27:25). Forty years later, judgment came upon that entire generation (Matt. 11:16; 12:39, 41-42, 45) when Jerusalem and the second temple were utterly destroyed in AD 70 as Jesus had predicted (Luke 21:5-6, 20-24) and hundreds of thousands were killed by the Romans.

Even while Jerusalem was being destroyed, many individuals were kept safe, including some of the apostles and disciples. Similarly, the Jewish leadership of Israel today (including religious Jews) does not embrace Jesus as Messiah, but individual Jews are being saved through their faith in Jesus. So, as we discuss the state of national Israel, let's remember that while people may be judged according to their nation, individuals who become followers of Jesus the Messiah will be saved from these trials. It's also important to remember that even in the first century, Paul loved his Jewish brethren but was bold enough to tell them they were lost and in need of salvation (Rom. 9:1-5; 10:1-5). We should do the same today.

An Honest Question Seeking Understanding of National Israel

I receive questions from people around the world every single day. I recently received the following question from a woman I'll call Cheryl. She wrote:

> I have some friends who go to a national denominational church. When I talk to them about prophecy and the nation of Israel, they say that the remaining promises to Israel were given to the church because of Israel's disobedience and murder of Jesus. They also point out that the modern nation of Israel is far from perfect. It is socialistic, secular, promotes LGBTQ, and is unfriendly to Messianic Christians. They ask me how I can support such a godless nation that rejects Jesus and hinders Christian evangelism. What can I say?

I responded as follows:

> There are two ways to respond to this question. One is theological and the other is prophetic. First, it is wise to simply acknowledge the truth of the assertions of your friends about the modern state of national Israel. It is well known that it was founded by secularist socialists who flirted with communism. If you study the history, many of the religious Jews were against the founding of the state of Israel because the founding fathers of modern Israel were so secular and atheistic. This was blasphemous to the religious Jews of the nineteenth and twentieth centuries.
>
> Second, we might ask the question, "In some ways how is this any different than the original founding of the nation in the Book of Exodus?" Notice what God says to Israel through Moses as they are about to enter the Promised Land: "Do not say in your heart, after the LORD your God has thrust them out before you, 'It is because of my righteousness that the LORD has brought me in to possess this land,' whereas it is because of the wickedness of these nations that the LORD is driving them out before you. *Not because of your righteousness or the uprightness of your heart* are you going in to possess their land, but because of the wickedness of these nations the LORD your God is driving them out from before you, and that *he may confirm the word that the Lord swore to your fathers, to Abraham, to Isaac, and to Jacob.* Know, therefore, that the LORD your God is not giving you this good land to possess *because of your righteousness, for you are a stubborn people.* Remember and

do not forget how you provoked the LORD your God to wrath in the wilderness. From the day you came out of the land of Egypt until you came to this place, you have been rebellious against the LORD. Even at Horeb you provoked the LORD to wrath, and the LORD was so angry with you that he was ready to destroy you" (Deut. 9:4–8 [emphasis added]).

Theologically, we learn that *God did not give the land to Israel in ancient times because they were righteous, but to keep His promises to the patriarchs.* Prophetically speaking, Israel today does not deserve the land any more than they did in ancient times. God did not bring back the people of Israel to the land in 1948 because they earned it (Ezek. 36:24; 38:8). He brought them back into the land so He can fulfill His prophetic promises of the seventieth week spoken of by Daniel (9:24–27), among other prophecies. He is going to judge them for their rebellion against His Son, Jesus, purge and discipline them, but save the remnant as they call out on the name of Jesus at the end of the tribulation (Jer. 30:7; Hos. 5:15; Matt. 23:37–39; Zech. 12:10; 13:8–9).

SHOULD CHRISTIANS SUPPORT THE STATE OF ISRAEL?

Why should we support the state of Israel today? We do not endorse everything they do. They are far from perfect as a government and a people. We support and love the state of Israel indirectly in a sense. Indirectly because we do not approve of them implicitly. More accurately, we support and endorse the Word of God, which contains promises to the nation of Israel that are still unfulfilled. Not a single time in Scripture are the promises to Israel ever transferred to the church. These promises will be fulfilled literally. Ultimately, we support and affirm the prophetic promises of God to and about Israel. God does not fully approve of Israel's actions today, and neither should we, but God has not forsaken nor abandoned Israel (Jer. 31:35–37; Amos 9:8; Rom. 11:25–29), and again, neither should we.

It is absolutely true what Jesus said, that no one can be saved apart from faith in Him (John 14:6; cf. Acts 4:12). It is pretty obvious that *secular* Jews anywhere in the world today are not saved. What about religious Jews who pray, read the Bible, and are waiting for the Messiah? Paul writes with great sorrow that *any* Jew who *does not embrace Jesus is lost* and unsaved (Rom. 10:1–3). Today, many religious Jews (especially in Israel) hate Jesus and Christians, sometimes aggressively.

That is how I answered Cheryl's question, and I believe it is a fitting response to the question of how we as Christians who follow Jesus as the Messiah and final sacrifice should address the prophetic developments of the red heifer and the building of the third temple.

WHAT ABOUT RELIGIOUS JEWS WHO PRAY TODAY?

I often get asked about those religious Jews who read and believe the Old Testament. They claim to pray to God the Father and also believe that His promises are true, but they reject Jesus as Messiah. We should always be friendly and loving and kind, and never are we to persecute or speak evil of anyone who does not embrace Jesus as Messiah. This is especially true of Jewish people, considering the history of "Christian" persecution of the Jews, which has always been and will always be wrong.

At the same time, we should consider a few questions:

- When Jewish people who reject Jesus as Messiah pray, does God the Father hear their prayers?

- Can a Jewish person have a relationship with God the Father if they reject Jesus?

- Are the Jewish people, who seem sincere in their desire to build a third temple, pleasing God if they are trying to please Him apart from faith in Jesus?

- Is Judaism a genuine religion that God accepts?

These are all very good questions, and the New Testament speaks quite boldly on these issues. In fact, as we have seen, Jesus speaks clearly on this issue. He said to the apostles and to Israel in the first century, "I am the way, the truth, and the life. No one comes to the Father except through me" (John 14:6). Peter said, "And there is salvation in no one else, for there is no other name under heaven given among men by which we must be saved" (Acts 4:12).

These are powerful and crystal-clear biblical answers to the above questions. As difficult as it may be for some to accept, the answer to all four of the questions above is an unequivocal "no."

A true and genuine religion is one that provides salvation, and any religion that does not embrace Jesus is false and cannot offer salvation. I do not intend for this to sound harsh, but it is true. Judaism, as a religion, does not and cannot provide salvation because it rejects the Messiah, Jesus. Therefore, all the efforts of the religious Jews to fully reestablish Judaism and the third temple sacrifices are fruitless and do not honor the Son. God cannot lie and accept their efforts when they reject His one and only Son, whom He gave to die for the sins of the Jews first and then for the Gentiles (Rom. 1:16).

So, when a religious Jew prays, his prayers are not accepted by the Father unless they are prayed in the context of having a relationship with Jesus, which many religious Jews clearly do not. Jesus said, "Whatever you ask in my name, this I will do, that the Father may be glorified in the Son" (John 14:13; see also 15:16; 16:23, 24, 26).

Notice the consistent theme of the following verses:

- John 3:17-18: "For God did not send his Son into the world to condemn the world, but in order that the world might be saved through him. Whoever believes in him is not condemned, but whoever does not believe is condemned already, because he has not believed in the name of the only Son of God."

- John 3:35-36: "The Father loves the Son and has given all things into his hand. Whoever believes in the Son has eternal life; whoever does not obey the

Son shall not see life, but the wrath of God remains on him."

- John 5:23: "That all may honor the Son, just as they honor the Father. Whoever does not honor the Son does not honor the Father who sent him."

- John 15:23: "Whoever hates me hates my Father also."

- Luke 10:16 (NASB): "The one who listens to you listens to Me, and the one who rejects you rejects Me; and he who rejects Me rejects the One who sent Me."

- 1 John 2:23 (NASB): "Whoever denies the Son does not have the Father; the one who confesses the Son has the Father also."

- John 5:45–46: "Do not think that I will accuse you to the Father. There is one who accuses you: Moses, on whom you have set your hope. For if you believed Moses, you would believe me; for he wrote of me."

- 1 John 2:21-23: "I write to you, not because you do not know the truth, but because you know it, and because no lie is of the truth. Who is the liar but he who denies that Jesus is the Messiah? This is the antichrist, he who denies the Father and the Son. No one who denies the Son has the Father. Whoever confesses the Son has the Father also."

- John 15:18–21: "If the world hates you, know that it has hated me before it hated you. If you were of the world, the world would love you as its own; but because you are not of the world, but I chose you out of the world, therefore the world hates you.

Remember the word that I said to you: 'A servant is not greater than his master.' If they persecuted Me, they will also persecute you. If they kept my word, they will also keep yours. But all these things they will do to you on account of my name, because they do not know him who sent me."

- Matthew 10:40: "Whoever receives you receives Me, and whoever receives me receives him who sent me."

- John 12:48-49: "The one who rejects me and does not receive my words has a judge; the word that I have spoken will judge him on the last day. For I have not spoken on my own authority, but the Father who sent me has himself given me a commandment—what to say and what to speak."

- Luke 12:8-9: "And I tell you, everyone who acknowledges me before men, the Son of Man also will acknowledge before the angels of God, but the one who denies me before men will be denied before the angels of God."

- 1 John 5:1 (NASB): "Whoever believes that Jesus is the Christ [Messiah] is born of God."

- 1 John 4:15 (NET): "If anyone confesses that Jesus is the Son of God, God resides in him and he in God."

These verses present a stark and clear picture of the situation in the first century as well as today when it comes to the Jewish people—or anyone at all, for that matter. It is impossible to honor the Father through prayer, Torah study, sacrifices, or building a third temple if it does not include honoring Jesus the Son. A person cannot know the Father without honoring Jesus as Messiah. In addition, if anyone rejects Jesus, they reject the Father who sent Jesus. If someone hates Jesus, they hate the Father.

Even more bold, 1 John 2:21-23 above says that anyone who

denies Jesus as the Messiah is a liar and is associated with the spirit of the Antichrist. I believe when the Antichrist comes on the scene to deceive the Jews into making a covenant with him (Dan. 9:27), part of his covenant message will encourage the Jewish leadership to reaffirm their denial of Jesus as the Messiah.

When Paul was outlining the plan of God in seeking to reach the Gentiles, he wrote, "As far as the gospel is concerned, [the Jews] are enemies for your sake; but as far as election is concerned, they are loved on account of the patriarchs, for God's gifts and his call are irrevocable" (Rom. 11:28–29, NIV). This is important. Paul says that any Jewish person who rejects the gospel is an enemy in one sense, but God still loves them and has a plan for them in the future.

As Christians, we should love the Jewish people and pray for their eyes to be opened to God's only plan of salvation, which includes their coming to faith in Jesus. However, just because God loves them, it doesn't mean He will provide a separate way for them to come to Him. Jesus is the only way (John 14:6; Acts 4:12).

By keeping these truths in the back of our mind, we can begin to formulate some solid biblical answers to the three questions about the red heifer and the third temple that we discussed in the previous chapter.

My Answers to the Three Questions About the Red Heifer Movement

In the previous chapter many of our favorite prophecy teachers shared their thoughts and wisdom on the discussion about the red heifers and the third temple. I deliberately did not read their comments in full before I wrote my own thoughts on the issue. In this way, I am offering up my own thoughts with humility, not knowingly or specifically either contradicting or agreeing with the thoughts of my brothers.

I was excited to write my answers and see how they compared to those of other prophecy teachers, whether we agree or disagree. Either way, these are not salvation issues, so it is OK if we disagree on some of these minor points. I know all these brothers well, and we all understand the spiritual maturity inherent in agreeing to disagree on topics not related to salvation. My answers are as follows.

1. Should Christians be excited about the preparations being made for the building of the third temple and the ritual slaughter of the red heifer?

I would absolutely say *yes* to this question, but we always need to frame our answers carefully. For whatever reasons, Christians have been opinionated on this issue. I have conducted several interviews on this topic and have seen a varied response. Some get very passionate and even angry when someone answers in a way they do not like. It is good to be a person of conviction, but the fruit of the Spirit is gentleness (Gal. 5:23). We are commanded to have an answer to defend the faith, but to do it in a spirit of gentleness and respect (1 Pet. 3:15).

I have had the opportunity to write quite a bit lately on what the Olivet Discourse and the Book of Revelation say concerning the seven-year tribulation. When you list the characteristics of this time period as found in these texts, it can make people fearful. The tribulation will be a time of unprecedented destruction upon the earth and the human race. Jesus said in Mark 13:19 that it will be the worst time in the history of the creation, including the flood. Jesus also said that if those days of judgment were not cut short, the entirety of humanity would perish (Matt. 24:22). Am I excited about this? No, I am not.

We know that the preparations for the red heifer ceremony and the coming third temple are attempts by religious Jews to seek after God apart from Jesus. They are trying to restore the Mosaic system of sacrifices that was ordained by God under the old covenant. They have rejected the sacrifice of Jesus and the institution of the new covenant through Him, which their own prophets foretold (Jer. 31:31-34; Ezek. 37:26).

In addition, the religious Jews will make an agreement with the Antichrist, which begins the seventieth week of Daniel (Dan. 9:27). They will receive him as the messiah (John 5:43) and be deceived into reinstituting the sacrificial system and the finalization of the third temple. This is moving backward! Instead, they should be receiving Jesus, who is greater than Moses (Heb. 3–4).

These actions will not please God, as we saw above. Yes, the religious Jews embrace the Mosaic covenant, but Jesus superseded that covenant. Therefore, the acts of embracing the old covenant and denying the sufficiency of the sacrifice of Jesus are blasphemous. Their efforts to build the third temple and slaughter the red heifer will not and cannot honor God because they do not honor His Son, Jesus, as we read in the verses above.

So, in conclusion, I am not excited about these events per se, but I am excited to see that the preparations being made serve as signs that Jesus is coming soon. He will first come to rapture away His saints and receive them to Himself, as He promised. Jesus told His disciples He was going to His Father's house (heaven) to prepare a place for us, and that He would come back one day and receive us to Himself, that we could go where He was going (John 14:1–3)! Now, that is a great and precious promise! So when I see preparations being made for the red heifer slaughter and the building of the third temple, this reveals to me that the rapture is coming very soon. That gets me excited!

2. Do you think God would approve of New Covenant Christians who are followers of Jesus financially contributing to the building of the third temple and the acquisition of a red heifer for Israel to ritually slaughter?

As a pastor and teacher for twenty-five years, I have been asked almost every biblical question you could imagine. My response is always to look for a verse that provides an authoritative answer. What does the Bible say? Or to frame this question another way, Is it a sin? If I say that something is a sin, then I need to have a Bible verse to back me up.

There is no specific verse in the Bible that prohibits a Christian from giving financially to the red heifer or third temple movements. So, that makes this a Romans 14 issue. Romans 14 discusses topics about which there is room for disagreement. In other words, this is not a salvation issue. We are to hold our opinions with love and respect toward our brothers or sisters who might disagree with us. We are not to judge them (Rom. 14:3-4, 10, 14).

Paul discussed issues that he did not see specifically written about in the Torah, the Old Testament in his day. He wrote, "'All things are lawful for me'—but not everything is beneficial. 'All things are lawful for me'—but I will not be controlled by anything" (1 Cor. 6:12, NET). Similarly he also wrote, "'All things are lawful,' but not all things are helpful. 'All things are lawful,' but not all things build up" (1 Cor. 10:23).

We learn several principles from these two passages. The Bible does not give answers to every last question, so Paul was saying that in one sense, all things were lawful for him. He obviously did not mean that murder or adultery or stealing was lawful, but that if the Bible did not specifically address something, it was OK for him to do. He did, however, mention some of his personal guidelines: 1) not everything is beneficial; 2) he would not do things that lead to addiction, or being controlled; and 3) not everything edifies or builds up others or himself.

Each person must come to their own conviction regarding this second question. Personally, I could not in good conscience donate financially to the red heifer movement nor to the third temple movement. Why? The main reason is that I would rather see my money go to ministries or missionary efforts proclaiming the gospel or teaching the New Covenant truths that clearly communicate that Jesus is the only way to salvation. That is my conviction; but I am not going to judge anyone else for their decision. That is between them and the Lord, as Romans 14:10 tells me.

CAN CHRISTIANS AND JEWS PRAY TOGETHER IN UNITY?

At the same time, I would like to address two issues I see coming on the horizon. Some Christians are advocating for and supporting the third temple movement out of a sincere desire for unity. They want to see peace and harmony among Jews, Christians, and Muslims on the Temple Mount. Shouldn't we all desire to see peace and harmony? Of course—but we must ask, at what cost? Jesus "was teaching them and saying to them, 'Is it not written, "My house shall be called a house of prayer for all the nations?" But you have made it a den of robbers'" (Mark 11:17; quote of Isaiah 56:7).

Some Christians believe that those who want to build the third temple are motivated by a desire to make it "a house of prayer for all nations" and fulfill Scripture. I think this is taking the passage out of context. At the time when Isaiah wrote this scripture, the Jews were commanded to be a light to the surrounding nations. Solomon also thought of the first temple as a house that could draw foreigners to worship the one true God (1 Kings 8:41-43). Sadly, Israel did not fulfill this vision, and by the time Jesus was on the earth, God had started a new age of gospel evangelization, one that did not involve a specific location (John 4:21-24).

This means any attempt to reestablish an old covenant temple system is an affront to the new covenant works that came through Jesus' death and resurrection. The veil of the second temple was torn from top to bottom, as we read earlier. The physical temple system era is over until Jesus builds a new temple during the Millennium (Ezek. 40-48).

Presently, the new and living way to access the holy of holies is through a relationship with Jesus, not by entering a physical temple (Heb. 10:19-21). Again, seeking to bring about unity through a physical temple administered by Jews under the old covenant is moving backward, especially for a Christian who should understand the theology found in the New Testament, specifically the Book of Hebrews.

Additionally, I am not sure how prayer would actually work in the third temple. Certainly the Jews would set up a holy of holies, an outer court, a women's court, and a court of the Gentiles far outside the inner precincts. They might invite a Gentile Christian to come pray in that outer court, but would they allow them to pray overtly in the name of Yeshua (Jesus)? This is highly doubtful.

Why would a Christian be content to pray in an outer court when we know that God has torn the veil to the holy of holies in two and we have access to the real holy of holies (Heb. 4:16; 7:19; 10:19; Eph. 3:12)? It seems contradictory and misleading. We would be pacifying our Jewish friends instead of letting them know in love that their efforts will not grant them salvation and participation in the world to come, the kingdom of heaven.

Can a Christian join together with a Jewish person or a Muslim and pray together in unity? This is impossible, as we would be committing blasphemy by implying that we all worship the same God. The Muslim denies that Allah has a son, and we know if you do not honor the Son, you do not honor the Father. This is also true of Judaism. They would say the God they worship does not have a divine son either, and they certainly reject Jesus. Jesus said that if anyone rejects Him, they are rejecting the Father whom they claim to worship (1 John 2:23). We cannot have it both ways.

One last comment: I have heard people assert that since Paul provided offerings in the second temple (Acts 21), this justifies the idea of a Christian making an offering in a future third temple. This is comparing apples to oranges. After God miraculously tore the veil of the second temple, He allowed a transition period of forty years, after which He destroyed that temple as a testimony of judgment against the Jewish leadership for murdering His Son. That second temple had been built by the prophets under the authority and commandment of God, and Jesus came and honored it with His presence. It had God-given authority, which slowly faded away until God removed it.

Today's efforts toward building a third temple were never commanded by an authoritative prophet of God and are being done in an overt rejection of the final sacrifice of Jesus. In fact, it is overt rebellion against Jesus and His message. It is apostasy. This is serious and quite different from what we find in the full context of Acts 21.

3. Would God providentially provide for the rebuilding of the temple and the procurement of the ashes of the red heifer?

I can answer this with an absolute *yes*. When we look at biblical history, we see that God has a grand plan that He works to accomplish. The story of Abraham in Genesis 16, for example, shows this to be true. God blessed Abraham with his wife, Sarah, and He also blessed Sarah by giving her Hagar as a servant. God did not cause Abraham to sin by sleeping with Hagar so she could bear him a son; Abraham did it without consulting God. God had given Hagar to Sarah in His sovereign kindness, but He did not endorse Abraham's actions with her.

God also providentially allowed the Ishmaelites to arrive at the exact time that Joseph was in the pit. They took Joseph to Egypt, and God raised him up to the second highest position in Egypt. God had not caused Joseph's brothers to throw him in the pit in order to sell him into slavery, but Joseph says in Genesis 50:20 that what they meant for evil, God meant for good.

As another example, God gave the Israelites gold and silver as they left and plundered Egypt (Exod. 3:22; 12:36). Yet they made the choice to use this same gold, which was a gift from God, for evil by making the golden calf (Exod. 32).

If we look at modern history we find many stories of miracles that took place during Israel's 1948 war of independence as well as the Six-Day War of 1967. Does this mean that God endorses all of modern Israel's behavior because He continues to protect them? It does not. It means God has a greater purpose in mind—the salvation of Israel toward the end of the seventieth week of Daniel. God miraculously brought them back to their land and continues to rescue them from all the enemies surrounding them to this day.

God is working out His sovereign, providential plan in order to bring the Jewish people into the tribulation period so He can discipline them and bring them to faith and salvation through His Son, Jesus, whom they will look upon and weep (Zech. 12:10). I see the red heifers and other opportunities as being providentially given in order to accomplish God's greater plan of salvation. They are still responsible and must repent of these efforts and receive Jesus as their Savior and Messiah.

Chapter 12

SOME COMMON QUESTIONS

THROUGHOUT THE LAST few years of writing, teaching, and conducting interviews about the red heifers, I have received many good questions and think it would be helpful to bring them together in one location.

DO YOU THINK THE RED HEIFER CEREMONY HAS ALREADY BEEN PERFORMED IN SECRET?

I have often considered the possibility of a secret red heifer ceremony and wondered whether it was possible. For two specific reasons, I don't think the ceremony has taken place in secret. The first relates to comments made in the *Daily Wire* article I referenced earlier, in chapter 8. Notice this quote:

> Conducting a red heifer ceremony is controversial in rabbinic circles, and there is far from a consensus over whether it can even be done, according to the Temple Institute, which provides rabbinical supervision for the cows.
>
> "There is no plan right now for using a kosher red heifer, killing it and turning it into ashes," Yitzchak Reuven, the director of international development for the Temple Institute told *The Daily Wire*. "Anyone saying this is making it up. We will only do this when the time is right, because there is no point in doing it if the Jewish and rabbinic world won't accept it."[1]

I find these quotes a little strange because the Temple Institute—along with the Boneh Israel organization—spent considerable time and resources searching for a qualified red heifer. Rabbis from the

Temple Institute visited Texas to give a preliminary inspection and then spent $700,000 to purchase and fly the five cows over to Israel.[2] Why would they do this if they were not prepared to officiate the ceremony? Either they were originally quite zealous to perform the ceremony and have since changed their minds, or else we are missing another piece of information.

The second reason why I believe the ceremony could not be done in secret relates to the geography of the precise locations on the Mount of Olives. (See chapter 5.) If you look at that map, you will see that these two locations are within the boundaries of eastern Jerusalem and hardly in a remote location. We must remember that the red heifer ritual ceremony essentially involves a large bonfire that could not be hidden in such a populated area. A fire of this size would produce major amounts of smoke and attract the attention of the fire department and police. In addition, ever since Hamas brought attention to the red cows in January 2024, the Arab people are also aware of these developments.

SOME PEOPLE SUGGEST THAT THE RED HEIFERS CURRENTLY IN SHILOH ARE JUST DECOYS. IS THIS TRUE?

Back in the fall of 2023 I had the opportunity to interview Byron Stinson. He was preparing various logistics for the red heifer ceremony, which was potentially planned for April or June of 2024. Obviously when this window passed, they did not suggest another time frame.

During that interview, I asked Byron about the security situation. These are expensive cows, and I assumed they would be kept in a secure environment that cannot be accessed by the public. Why? Well, remember that any small action can disqualify the cows. They do not have to be killed to be disqualified; they just need to be blemished by a small cut or a brand. Even throwing an object like a blanket or a yoke over a cow could disqualify it.

I had a couple of friends visit the Shiloh visitor center in June 2024. They were so close to the five red cows that the animals were licking my friend's hand. Obviously this is not tight security by any stretch of the imagination. For this reason, I am skeptical that the real qualified cows from Texas are accessible to the public at Shiloh. It seems likely that at least a few of them are decoys. I do not know for sure and this is just my guess, but looking at the situation logically, it makes sense.

How many red heifers are still qualified?

Based on the latest news from December 2024, only two red heifers of the original five flown to Israel in September 2022 remain preliminarily qualified. Remember that any cow that is preliminarily qualified must be examined and requalified immediately prior to the ceremony.

Is there an upper limit on the age of the red heifer?

According to the Temple Institute website, there is no maximum age limit for the red heifer. There are many diverse opinions on this matter among the rabbis, but the following is an official statement from the Temple Institute website.

> As for the time the red heifer may be used for this commandment—the Sages state that it is valid when it reaches maturity, i.e. from the beginning of its third year. *From this age and onward the red heifer is valid without age limitations.* Though, ideally, one should not wait till it passes the age of four, lest it grows hairs of colors that deem it invalid.[3]

Does the red heifer need to be born in Israel?

See chapter 5, especially the story of the Gentile named Damah ben (son of) Netinah. The answer is no, it does not.

Can the red heifer be genetically modified?

Opinions among the rabbis vary on this issue, but efforts have been made in the past to import Red Angus cow embryos for the sake of the Israel red heifer breeding program. It also depends on how someone might define "genetically modified" with its various nuances.

WHAT WILL BE DONE WITH THE DISQUALIFIED RED HEIFERS?

While the five red heifers flown to Israel in 2022 were quite costly, we can be assured that any cow that becomes disqualified will not simply become an expensive steak. Those that are disqualified will be used in the Israeli breeding program, as they still maintain superb genetics to pass on to the next generation.

WHAT IS THE NEXT WINDOW FOR THE RED HEIFERS TO BE USED IN A CEREMONY? IS THE RED HEIFER CEREMONY IMMINENT?

The increased interest in the upcoming red heifer ceremony is positive in that it has drawn more people into the understanding that we are living at the end of the age. The negative part is that misinformation seems to be ubiquitous on the internet. I've also observed a great amount of carelessness or even intentional misleading by so-called journalists when covering news about the red heifer.

Consider one example. In March 2024, CBS news correspondent Chris Livesay went to Israel to report on the red heifers that are now in Shiloh. He interviewed Yitshak Mamo, a rabbi affiliated with the Temple Institute who owns a piece of property on the Mount of Olives where the ceremony will likely take place. In the interview Livesay intimated that the efforts of Mamo and others involved in bringing the red heifers to Israel had caused the October 7 Hamas attack. It seemed quite obvious to me in the video accompanying the article that he was providing incendiary material with a Palestinian bias.[4] He also stated in the video that "a massive altar already awaits where the heifers are to be burned," and the CBS clip showed an image (at the 2:03 mark) of a large white ramp structure surrounded by an industrial area and green Astroturf.[5]

At least three things are wrong with this report. First, this altar is in the West Bank and not on the Mount of Olives, which is the required ceremony location according to the rabbinic tradition of the Mishnah. Second, the ceremony does not involve an altar. In the third temple system, the only altar that exists is on the Temple Mount. The red heifer is not to be sacrificed, as sacrifices only happen on the Temple Mount; it is to be slaughtered and then burned whole on a pyre with other elements as described in Numbers 19. Third, this altar has since been torn down and is no longer used for rehearsals. Yet the CBS report made it look like this altar is currently being built for the very purpose of the red heifer ceremony. I can't help but think this was an attempt to inflame the situation with the Arab population and foment increased hostility against the Jewish people and the red heifer/third temple movement.

The red heifers showed up in the news again with exaggerated fanfare. This time it involved a rehearsal ceremony with a picture of a cow next to a rabbi and a priest with several other people. The tweet, written in Hebrew, said, "Towards Tisha B'Av: Temple worshipers are now practicing the mitzvah of a red cow in front of the Temple Mount, which will enable the return of purity and the observance of all the temple mitzvahs."[6]

While there was nothing wrong with his report, there were several elements in the picture that I found humorous. One, in the background it showed a paper cutout of a red heifer that was not even fully red! Second, the image included a rabbi named Azaria Ariel, who is the research director at the Temple Institute organization and the son of the founder of the institute. Third, this practice rehearsal was taking place in the old city not far from the Western Wall and the Temple Mount. In the picture you could clearly see the Mount of Olives in the background and the Dome of the Rock on the Temple Mount. So, this practice ceremony was clearly not happening at the required location of the Mount of Olives.

I do not fault the sincerity in those involved in this rehearsal, as they were simply practicing with what appeared to be a young priest. However, many people ran to social media and posted that a new red heifer ceremony was taking place right now in Israel! This was a complete lie and pure exaggeration. Nothing of the sort was true. We always need to do our research and vet information before passing it along, recognizing that much of what is being presented these days is completely erroneous.

At the same time, we realize that the delay in performing the ceremony on the Mount of Olives does not mean that those involved in the process are standing idly by. They continue to practice the ceremony, and it remains prominent in their current thinking. Numerous groups of rabbis are working out the details and trying to gain as much consensus as possible among the various religious orthodox groups.

One last item to note is that Aaron Lipkin (of Lipkin Israel tours) visited the site in Shiloh in July 2024 and recorded a video.[7] He mentioned that three of the cows had been officially disqualified, leaving only two that maintain a level of preliminary qualification. The rabbis have been quick to say that the cows cannot be fully qualified until the moment before the ceremony takes place. Until then, it is only preliminary, as the rabbis will need to do a fresh evaluation immediately before the ceremony takes place.

We are living in exciting times, as we haven't seen even a preliminarily qualified red heifer in nineteen hundred years! Jesus is coming soon, and He will fix the world and all its mess. The world will be filled with the glory of the Lord as the waters cover the sea (Hab. 2:14). God's presence will no longer be in the shadows, and the whole world will give Him the rightful glory He deserves.

WHY IS THE THIRD TEMPLE CALLED THE "TEMPLE OF GOD"?

I often receive an extended version of this question that says, "If God did not want the Jews to build the temple that will be present in the tribulation, then why are these temples referred to as the 'temple of God'?"

There are several ways to think through this question. First, we know that Jesus is the final sacrifice and no other physical temple is needed in this current age. Therefore, in an immediate sense,

God does not want the Jews to build a temple. For the Jewish people to return to Moses and the Law instead of receiving Jesus as the Messiah and accepting His completed work would be a step backward. Yet, in order to bring them to ultimate salvation (Rom. 11:26), God will providentially ordain them to build this temple so their trust in the Antichrist will be shattered, which is one reason for the tribulation period (Jer. 30:7; Dan. 12:7). Bible teachers often label this as a distinction between the *prescriptive* will of God and His *providential* or *permissive* will. God will use this false third temple and their agreement with the Antichrist to break the stubborn will of the Jewish people during the seven-year tribulation as He brings them back to Himself and they ultimately call upon the name of Jesus (Matt. 23:37-39; Hos. 5:15; Deut. 9:6).

A second consideration about the use of "the temple *of God*" in 2 Thessalonians 2:4 and Revelation 11:1 revolves around the technical use of the Greek noun *theou*, found in the genitive case, which indicates possession or association. The genitive case is the specific form of nouns in the Greek New Testament. In Daniel Wallace's book *Greek Grammar Beyond the Basics*, he labels one use of the genitive case as a "genitive of association."[8] In other words, the temple is not actually "of God," endorsed by God with its false sacrifices, but instead could be translated "the temple *associated with* God," and this certainly fits the context of both passages.

A third consideration is that God said quite clearly in Old Testament texts that the Temple Mount is where He would put His *name* (2 Kings 21:7). Yahweh owns the Temple Mount. It is where Abraham almost sacrificed his son Isaac in Genesis 22. It is the place where David purchased the threshing floor (2 Sam. 24:18). Though the Jews are currently in a state of unbelief, the very possession of the location itself could lend to the idea that any temple there would be considered sanctified in some sense—not in a salvation sense, as we see in 1 Corinthians 7:14 where an unbelieving spouse and child are sanctified (set apart) by the believing spouse.

I prefer the second option above, but as you can see, there are various ways to understand the use of "the temple of God" in the New Testament.

Chapter 13

Concluding Thoughts on the Red Heifer Movement

WHERE DO WE go from here? I set out as my goal to provide the reader with a definitive book that lays out a biblical framework for understanding current prophetic developments that connect with the red heifers and the third temple. Even though a number of red heifers have appeared throughout recent years, the biggest news yet was the arrival of five potential candidates in the land of Israel in September 2022. We now know that only two candidates remain qualified in a preliminary sense as 2024 comes to a close.

Even if all five red heifers should eventually become disqualified, the religious Jews have made tremendous progress in preparing for the construction of a third temple, and they most certainly will continue their efforts to find a qualified red heifer to slaughter in their ritual. I hope that when the day of the red heifer slaughter comes and passes, this book will still provide a background and framework for understanding what has occurred as well as a solid biblical Christian response to the event.

After nearly two thousand years, we certainly seem to be on the cusp of Bible prophecy in the seventieth week of Daniel. We are witnessing the preparations being set in place for the purification of the Temple Mount and construction of a third temple, which thereby sets the stage for events in the seven-year tribulation. We live in exciting times—and heartbreaking times; it is exciting to realize we may be the generation to witness the Lord's return but heartbreaking to consider the deception, persecution, and destruction that are coming on the earth. Jesus wept over Jerusalem as He predicted its destruction due to the Jews' rejection of His offer of salvation (Luke 19:41-44; 21:21-24; 23:37-41).

Just as Jesus wept over the situation in the first century, we should reflect the same somber attitude at what is coming for our Jewish friends who have not yet received Jesus as Messiah during the coming seventieth week of Daniel. It is called *the time of Jacob's trouble*, and it certainly will be a time of great distress (Jer. 30:7; Mark 13:19).

So, how should we prepare now? Most importantly we need to be ready and equipped to answer questions and evangelize those around us as to the prophetic signs happening every day. We know the Lord wants us to always be ready to give a reason for the hope that we have (1 Pet. 3:15). As the world continues getting worse and people grow weary (2 Tim. 3:13), we can take hope and comfort in knowing that Jesus has already won the war and look forward to the day when Jesus will return for His bride.

As we are seeing prophecy fulfilled in our time, let us not forget that we are all sinners (Rom. 3:23) and none of us is perfect (Rom. 3:10). The penalty for our sin is death; we all deserve it (Rom. 6:23). That is the bad news. But isn't it marvelous that God gave us the good news! God showed His love to us in that while we were still sinners, Jesus died in our place (Rom. 5:8). If we repent of our sins and ask Him to forgive and save us, we can be confident that we will escape the coming seven-year tribulation as well as eternal judgment (Rom. 10:9; 1 Thess. 1:10; 5:9; Rom. 5:9). I encourage you to continue to seek the Lord and to remain steadfast and prepared for His return.

May the Lord bless you as you seek Him. I encourage you to check out Prophecy Watchers (prophecywatchers.com) and our podcast at TheWeekInBibleProphecy.com, where we will continue to keep you informed and updated on the prophetic times in which we live.

Jesus said,

> And what I say to you, I say to all: Watch!
> —MARK 13:37, NKJV

Appendix A

Second Thessalonians 2:3— A Jewish Apostasy or Church Apostasy?

THE APOSTLE PAUL wrote to the church at Thessalonica:

> Let no one deceive you in any way. For that day will not come, unless the rebellion comes first, and the man of lawlessness is revealed, the son of destruction.
> —2 Thessalonians 2:3

The topic of whether to watch for a Jewish apostasy or a church apostasy has been on my mind for quite some time. If we do not accurately interpret this section of Scripture, there will be ramifications. It contributes to our understanding of the timing of the rapture, the nature and start of the day of the Lord, the arrival of the Antichrist, the coming apostasy, and navigating the waters of potential pretribulation church persecution. In addition, other technical details in the Greek contribute to one's understanding about the transition between the church age and the start of the tribulation.

Before jumping into 2 Thessalonians 2, let us review the context and history of Paul's interactions with the church at Thessalonica in order to establish confidence in our interpretation of this text.

After Paul was beaten and imprisoned in Philippi, he departed and went to the city of Thessalonica (Acts 17:1-12). He preached there for only three sabbaths, which could mean as little as fifteen days or as many as twenty-seven days of teaching the

Thessalonians about the gospel, including prophecies related to Jesus' second coming.

The important element to recognize here is that Paul did not stay in Thessalonica long after he established the church. Even in that short time, Paul shared the fundamentals of the gospel and also taught them vital elements of eschatology, as well as complex details about the nature of the Antichrist and the future tribulation period (2 Thess. 2:5). This should speak volumes to those pastors who do not feel eschatology is important enough to teach new believers.

It is important that we understand the frame of mind of the Thessalonian believers. From the beginning, since the time of its founding their church was surrounded by controversy and resistance. After Paul had been physically assaulted and imprisoned in Philippi, he came to the synagogue at Thessalonica, preaching about Jesus. Many of the Thessalonians also came to believe under the threat of persecution themselves, which they eventually suffered. We know this is true because Paul wrote his first epistle to them not long after he had left. Paul wrote, "And you became imitators of us and of the Lord, for you received the word in much affliction, with the joy of the Holy Spirit" (1 Thess. 1:6).

We also read that Paul was concerned about the Thessalonians' new faith and sent Timothy back to check on them. Paul reminded them to stay true to Christ in the midst of hardship. He instructed them, "that no one be moved by these afflictions. For you yourselves know that we are destined for this. For when we were with you, we kept telling you beforehand that we were to suffer affliction, just as it has come to pass, and just as you know" (1 Thess. 3:3-4; see also 1 Thess. 2:14; 3:7).

When we come to Paul's second epistle to the Thessalonians, we learn that they were still suffering afflictions and persecutions. Paul says, "Therefore we ourselves boast about you in the churches of God for your steadfastness and faith in all your persecutions and in the afflictions that you are enduring" (2 Thess 1:4). We can fairly say that two prominent themes in the Thessalonian epistles are understanding the coming "day of the Lord" and how to persevere in suffering and affliction. This helps us understand the background of 2 Thessalonians 2 more specifically.

Before we outline the section that interests us for the purpose of this appendix—2 Thessalonians 2:1-12—it is wise to remember that Paul addressed the theological truth that the church will not be subject to the eschatological wrath to come (1 Thess. 1:10; 5:9). The wrath in context is clearly a reference to the day of the Lord (which from here on I will refer to using the acronym DOTL), also known as the seven-year tribulation (1 Thess. 5:2-9). This is one of the many reasons I believe in a pretribulation rapture. Paul teaches believers to "wait for his Son from heaven, whom he raised from the dead, Jesus who *delivers us from the wrath to come*" (1 Thess. 1:10, emphasis added).

After encouraging the Thessalonians that they did not need any more instruction about the times and seasons, Paul again comforts them (5:1, 11). He tells them that the unbelieving world, which is saying "peace and safety," will not escape judgment. He specifically says that this judgment will come upon *them* (the wicked), which denotes that it will not come upon the church.

Since we are children of the light, we will always be ready for His return. It is with this encouragement that we know in addition to being *delivered* from the wrath to come (1:10), we are saved from the future seven-year tribulation, the DOTL, as Paul writes, "But since we belong to the day, let us be sober, having put on the breastplate of faith and love, and for a helmet the hope of salvation. For God *has not destined us for wrath*, but to obtain salvation through our Lord Jesus Christ" (1 Thess. 5:8-9, emphasis added). It is no surprise, then, to acknowledge that Paul wrote about the details of the rapture in 1 Thessalonians 4:13-18, which is clearly *before* he discussed the DOTL in chapter 5.

Think back to when you were a new believer. You were learning about the many doctrines of the Bible. Now, add on some persecution and affliction because of your new faith. It is a lot to take in. This was the situation with the Thessalonians. In addition, Paul had been teaching them about the rescue of the rapture prior to the DOTL, the arrival of the Antichrist and his coming to the temple in Jerusalem, and the increased worldwide trouble and affliction.

Things were getting even more intense for them, and this led to much confusion. For example, in 1 Thessalonians 4:13-18, Paul clarifies some issues concerning the rapture. They thought their loved ones who had become believers and died would miss out on the rapture. They were grieved over this. Instead, Paul taught them that those who died would not miss out on the rapture but in fact would be raised from the dead first.

This same type of confusion occurred a second time. Paul received word that the Thessalonian believers were still confused about details concerning the rapture and the start of the DOTL. Since they continued undergoing persecution, they began to hear rumors from an unknown source that the DOTL had started and that they were in it. Naturally, this would have confused the Thessalonians, since Paul had told them they would be raptured prior to the start of the DOTL. Paul chose to write them another letter of encouragement (2 Thessalonians) to remind them of details that he had already taught them (2 Thess. 2:5).

The summary of the section, 2:1-3, goes like this: The main point Paul seeks to correct is the confusion about the end of the age scenario. In verse 1 he brings up the rapture ("our gathering together to Him," NKJV), letting them know he understands why they are confused. He also asks them not to be shaken or alarmed that the DOTL was already present (2:2). In verse 3 he reminds them not to be deceived and that the DOTL could not be present because the apostasy and the revelation of the Antichrist had not yet occurred.

Then, in verse 4, Paul discusses the act of the Antichrist declaring himself to be god in the temple itself. He then reminds them in verse 5 that he had already explained these things to them. Verses 6-8 discuss the work of the restrainer and how the Antichrist will be revealed. Verses 9-12 discuss the supernatural arrival and work of the Antichrist and the deception that will ensue because people reject the gospel and the truth.

Now that we have covered the background and introduction, it will be helpful to zoom in on some specifics in 2 Thessalonians 2:1-3. If we do not see the flow of these verses, we will be confused as we discuss the details of verse 3 concerning the meaning of the apostasy. Let's proceed through this one verse at a time, with some commentary.

Second Thessalonians 2:1: "Now concerning the coming of our Lord Jesus Christ and our being gathered together to him, we ask you, brothers..."

Just prior to 2:1, Paul had been speaking in general terms about the revealing of Jesus and the day of His coming (1:7, 10). In 2:1, he transitions to specifics about the relationship between the rapture and the day of the Lord's arrival. As we see in 2:5, all these things in verses 1-4 Paul had previously taught them either in written form (the epistle of 1 Thessalonians) or in person, or both.

It is crystal clear in 2:1 that Paul brings up the topic of the rapture. This intimate language of "being gathered together to him" is reminiscent of John 14:1-3 ("receive you to Myself," NKJV) as well as 1 Thessalonians 4:17 ("and so we shall always be with the Lord," NASB). Both of these passages are a clear reference to the concept of the rapture. The final thing to note in this verse is that Paul stands posed to ask a question of the Thessalonian believers that connects with the rapture.

Second Thessalonians 2:2 (NET): "...not to be easily shaken from your composure or disturbed [frightened] by any kind of spirit or message or letter allegedly from us, to the effect that the day of the Lord is already here [present]."

Paul poses a question starting with verse 1, asking the Thessalonians not to be shaken or frightened as if the DOTL were already present. Why would they think the DOTL was already present? Two things could have contributed to this error: The first is that a rumor had come to Thessalonica that the DOTL had come. Paul was not sure whether this rumor began through someone claiming a spiritual revelation, through an oral message, or through a written letter he had allegedly sent.

The second thing that may have misled the Thessalonian believers and caused them to become frightened was the fact that they were still experiencing tremendous affliction. These two items caused the Thessalonians to become worried, frightened, and alarmed. Paul writes to them, asking them not to lose their composure nor to think that the DOTL was already present. They were scared out of their minds that they were inside the DOTL, and he wanted to encourage them that this was not the case. In fact, he indicated that they should have known better based on his previous teachings (cf. 2:5).

Before moving on from verse 2, one extremely important phrase must be addressed, and it has to do with the *last words* of the verse. The English Standard Version and New American Standard Bible say "to the effect that the day of the Lord *has come*" (emphasis added). A more literal translation, found in most exegetical commentaries, says, "to the effect that the day of the Lord is *already present*." The NET Bible reads, "not to be easily shaken from your composure or disturbed by any kind of spirit or message or letter allegedly from us, to the effect that the day of the Lord is already here."

The Greek word here for *already present* is *enesteken*. If we compare this with other Pauline writings, it becomes crystal clear that the best translation for this Greek word would be the English word "present" (Rom. 8:38; 1 Cor. 3:22; 7:26; Gal. 1:4; Heb. 9:9). Paul writes, "For I am sure that neither death nor life, nor angels nor rulers, nor things *present* nor things to come, nor powers..." (Rom. 8:38, emphasis added); also, "whether Paul or Apollos or Cephas or the world or life or death or *the present* or the future—all are yours" (1 Cor. 3:22, emphasis added). Paul later writes, "I think that in view of *the present* distress it is good for a person to remain as he is" (1 Cor. 7:26, emphasis added). For completeness, let me quote the last two instances. Galatians 1:4 says, "who gave himself for our sins to deliver us from *the present* evil age, according to the will of our God and Father" (emphasis added). Finally in Hebrews 9:9, the writer says, "(which is symbolic for *the present* age). According to this arrangement, gifts and sacrifices are offered that cannot perfect the conscience of the worshiper" (emphasis added).

Robert Thomas, in his article "The Rapture and the Biblical Teaching of Imminence" in the book *Evidence for the Rapture*, discusses the importance of this word in interpreting 2 Thessalonians 2:1-3. He writes:

> The issue involved in his [Paul's] correction of the false information to which the readers [Thessalonians] had been exposed is not the *future* coming of the day of the Lord; it is rather the current *non-presence* of that day at the time he writes and they read his words. If that day were not present, then they could not be in that day.
>
> For example, suppose I say, "In the northern states, the fall season **will not come** unless *first* the weather gets colder and the tree leaves change their colors." This sentence might imply that the weather gets colder and the tree leaves change their colors *before* the fall season comes. But this isn't true. These changes do not occur *before* the fall but are *part* of the fall season. But if I say, 'The fall season **is not present** (is not here) unless *first* the weather gets colder and the tree leaves change their colors," this implies something different. The cooler weather happens first, and then the colors of the leaves change. These two factors take place *within* the fall season and indicate its arrival. They don't occur *before* the fall season arrives.[1]

To summarize this important phrase, we are going to be discussing the apostasy (rebellion) coming first and the man of lawlessness being revealed (2:3). What this means is that the apostasy which arrives first and the man of sin being revealed happen *within* the seven-year tribulation period (DOTL) and do not *precede* or come *before* it, as many people think. Robert Thomas gives more grammatical evidence and parallels (John 7:51; Mark 3:27) in his article as to why these two items are considered to be *within* the tribulation period and *not outside* of it.

Let me belabor this point a little further. Some people interpret that the apostasy and man of sin must come *before* the arrival of the DOTL. This is unfortunate because the words *before* and *precede* do not appear anywhere in these verses. This erroneous interpretation leads some people to embrace a pre-wrath rapture view. For them, the rapture cannot happen until the apostasy and man of sin are revealed before the arrival of the DOTL. They have made a serious mistake. Paul never says that these two events happen before the arrival of the DOTL; he says they are the first events that kick off the DOTL.

In closing this section, it might be helpful to say that this translation of "already present" is not so unconventional. The NET Bible, from the scholars at Dallas Theological Seminary, is also closely worded but has the exact same meaning.

To summarize, Paul was saying that the Thessalonians should not be worried about the rumor that the DOTL was present. The DOTL could not be present because the first events of the DOTL had not yet happened, which he then explains in the following verses.

Second Thessalonians 2:2-3: "...not to be quickly shaken in mind or alarmed, either by a spirit or a spoken word, or a letter seeming to be from us, *to the effect that the day of the Lord [is already present]*. Let no one deceive you in any way. *For that day [is not present]*, unless the rebellion comes first, and the *man of lawlessness* is revealed, the son of destruction" (emphasis added).

One comment should be noted right up front that will help blunt the assertion that 2 Thessalonians 2:1-3 is evidence of a pre-wrath rapture. Some people recognize that the rapture (Greek, "gathering together," or *episynagō*) is being discussed in verse 1, and since verse 3 says *"that day"* cannot come unless the apostasy comes first and "the man of sin is revealed" (NKJV, emphasis added), they think this proves a mid-tribulation or pre-wrath position. However, "that day" does not refer to the day of the rapture of verse 1 but instead very specifically to the "day of the Lord" as found in verse 2. Paul introduces the rapture as an end-time event with the second coming of Jesus in verse 1, but then in verse 2 he specifically transitions to the topic of the DOTL. It makes great sense that he would introduce the topic of the rapture prior to discussing the DOTL and its beginning because the rapture precedes the start of the DOTL.

In verse 3 Paul is saying that the events that start the DOTL are the apostasy and the man of sin being revealed. When I took Greek and Hebrew classes in seminary, we would take complex Greek sentences and put them in the same order but in English. For example, the Thessalonians had become concerned that they were already inside the DOTL. Paul helped them to understand this was not true because they had not seen the rebellion happening nor the man of sin ("man of lawlessness") being revealed—the two specific *first* events inside the DOTL.

In a modern sense, let's say that someone was at a football party, became distracted by various things, and then started to freak out thinking they were missing out on the football game. I would say to them, "Do not be freaking out thinking that the game has already started, for the game cannot be here (present) unless the referee blows the whistle *first* and the kickoff happens." No one is going to say that the whistle occurs *before* the game begins or that the kickoff *precedes* the football game. These two events are exactly the very *first* events inside the game. They are part of the game, not something that happens before the game. In the same way, the apostasy and man of sin being revealed do not happen before the DOTL starts; they are the first events that kick off the DOTL.

So, what is *the* apostasy mentioned in 2:3, which is said to be the first event of the DOTL? There are three basic options of which the Greek word *apostasia* might refer.

1. Spiritual apostasy, falling away, or rebellion of the church

2. Spiritual apostasy, falling away, or rebellion of the Jewish people (national Israel)

3. The physical departure of the church at the rapture

Let's begin with number 3, which has been most prominently promoted by Andy Woods, PhD. He wrote a book back in 2018 titled *The Falling Away: Spiritual Departure or Physical Rapture? A Second Look at 2 Thessalonians 2:3*. In it he gave ten reasons he believes the first event to happen at the start of the DOTL will be the physical departure of the church (the rapture).[2] Woods also wrote an article in 2017 for the *Prophecy Watcher* magazine on this subject. One of the points he made in the article addressed the probability of the Greek word *apostasia* referring to a church apostasy. When I first read his comments criticizing this view (a church apostasy), I found it quite compelling—and I still do.

Woods wrote, "Spiritual departures are not abnormal. In fact, spiritual departures regularly transpire in Scripture going all the way back to the Fall of man as recorded in Genesis 3. The apostle Paul in his day even predicted a spiritual departure after he left (Acts 20:28-31)."[3] He then went on to provide many passages of Scripture showing various types of church apostasy at different times as listed in the New Testament.

Later in the article Woods discusses why he believes *apostasia* refers to a physical departure of the church (rapture). He commented:

> There is a definite article in front of the noun "apostasy." Second Thessalonians 2:3 says, "Let no one deceive you by any means; for that Day will not come unless the falling away comes first, and the man of sin is revealed, the son of perdition" (NKJV). Notice the definite article translated "the" in front of both "falling away" and "man of sin." By providing these two definite articles, essentially Paul is indicating that the apostasy will be something that has specific, time-bound qualities just like the man of sin's coming has such qualities. In other words, just like the advent of the man of sin will be a specific and instantaneous event in future history, the coming *apostasia*, or departure, will similarly be specific and time bound.[4]

The argument he presents here is that the definite articles make a specific point about the *apostasia* being something definite and not a nebulous church apostasy, which would be hard to prove, as it would not be a singular, time-bound event. If this were the case, how would we even know it happened? There is not one single person who speaks for the entire worldwide church. Maybe if we were Catholics and the Pope gave a pronouncement that the Catholic church was embracing Islam or something that heretical, it could be a specific, time-bound event. But we don't follow the authority of the Pope anyway.

Woods continues:

> The advent of the coming lawless one or Antichrist will take place at a specified point in time and instantaneously, with the opening of the first seal judgment (Rev. 6:1-2). The definite article before the word *apostasia*, indicates that the *apostasia* will also take place instantaneously. Such an instantaneous manifestation does not fit well with the notion of a spiritual departure, which typically transpires gradually over an elongated process.
>
> Spiritual departures are not instantaneous events. After all, it took the church at Ephesus three decades to spiritually depart from Christ by leaving its first love (Rev. 2:4-5). However, unlike gradual, spiritual departures, the rapture of the church will be an instantaneous event that will take place "in a moment, in the twinkling of an eye" (1 Cor. 15:51). Thus, the use of the two definite articles indicates that the *apostasia* will take place just as instantly as the coming forth of the lawless one. This understanding better harmonizes with interpreting "the *apostasia*" as the instantaneous removal of the church through the rapture rather than a gradual doctrinal erosion.[5]

I think Woods makes a compelling argument against the idea that *the apostasia* of 2 Thessalonians 2:3 can refer to a church apostasy. Not long after reading his comments, I came across a book by Lee Brainard called *Apostasia in 2 Thessalonians 2:3: Rapture or Apostasy?* in which he performed an extensive linguistic study and full refutation of the various arguments put forward by Dr. Woods.[6] After reading Lee's book, I found it quite persuasive in showing why the word *apostasia* does not mean a physical departure (rapture).

Now I found myself in a conundrum. Woods proved that *apostasia* could not refer to a church apostasy or rebellion, and Lee Brainard proved that *apostasia* could not refer to the rapture. This left only one main alternative: that the apostasy (spiritual rebellion) in this passage referred to a spiritual rebellion involving the Jewish people.

The title of this appendix and the question before us remains: Is this the spiritual apostasy of the church or of the Jews/Israel? The context of verse 2 and into verse 3 immediately preceding the apostasy is about the day of the Lord's arrival (also known as the seven-year tribulation period).

Here are some questions to ponder as we dive a little deeper into the DOTL.

1. What is the focus of the day of the Lord (Jer. 30:7; Dan. 9:24, 27; Hos. 5:15)?

2. What is the telltale sign that the seven-year tribulation has begun and is present (Dan. 9:27)?

3. Who is Jesus talking about in John 5:43? What does it mean for the Jews to receive this other person (as Messiah or Christ)?

4. When will the Jews receive this other person as Christ?

5. In 2 Thessalonians 2:3 it says *the* apostasy. If this is the apostasy of the *church*, how will we know exactly when it happens?

6. If 2 Thessalonians 2:3 refers to *the* apostasy of the *Jews*, how will we know exactly when it happens?

I think it would be helpful to interact with the previous questions one by one.

1. WHAT IS THE FOCUS OF THE DAY OF THE LORD?

Dispensational prophecy teachers believe that the primary focus of the DOTL is Israel. It is known as "the time of Jacob's trouble" (Jer. 30:7, NKJV). Indeed, the whole earth is involved and being judged (Rev. 3:10; Isa. 24:21), but we also know that the tribulation is the seventieth week of Daniel, which applies specifically to the

Jewish people and the holy city of Jerusalem (Dan. 9:24-27). It is important to note that the day of the Lord includes the seven-year tribulation period also known as the seventieth week of Daniel.

What are the purposes of the seven-year tribulation for Israel? These are outlined in Daniel 9:24-27.

- To finish the transgression, or rebellion (Dan. 9:24)

- To mark the ending of sin as a dominating influence (though there will still be sin in the thousand years)[7]

- To atone or cleanse the iniquity in Israel and Jerusalem

- To bring in everlasting righteousness (Dan. 2:44; Isa. 9:6-7)

- To seal (authenticate) vision and prophecy

- To anoint the most holy place (Ezek. 45:3)

A secondary purpose of the seven-year tribulation for Israel is that God will use this time to bring them to salvation by the end of the period in order to fulfill His promises. The list below describes some of the ways God will accomplish this.

- You will receive one who comes in his own name (the Antichrist; John 5:43).

- God will shatter the power of the people (Dan. 12:7).

- It will be the time of Jacob's trouble, but he will be saved out of it (Jer. 30:7).

- Two-thirds will be cut off; one-third will be refined. God answers their call (Zech. 13:8-9).

- Jesus said they will not see Him again until they call Him blessed (Matt. 23:37-39).

- "I will return again to my place, until they acknowledge their guilt and seek my face, and in their distress earnestly seek me" (Hos. 5:15).

As we meditate on Paul's words in 2 Thessalonians 2:1-4 and the specific context of the DOTL, it brings up some potential objections. Some people might object and say that Paul is providing the Thessalonian church with information about the apostasy of the future, end-time church. This is possible, but it interrupts the flow from what he started in verse 2, the DOTL. The church is not in the DOTL, so why would the apostasy be about the church? In fact, after introducing the two items in the beginning stages of the DOTL, he proceeds to describe the future activities of the Antichrist as polluting the temple of God, which we know is in Jerusalem (2:4). This is clearly a Jewish context and not a church context.

Others might object to a Jewish apostasy because they narrowly define the word *apostasy* in English. The *American Heritage Dictionary of the English Language* gives a basic definition. Their definition is "an abandonment of one's religious faith, a political party, one's principles, or a cause." Two other definitions from the GNU Collaborative International Dictionary of English definition are helpful. Their first definition is "an abandonment of what one has voluntarily professed"; the second is "a total desertion of departure from one's faith, principles, or party; esp., the renunciation of a religious faith."[8]

In his commentary on 1 and 2 Thessalonians, New Testament scholar Gordon Fee writes:

> Furthermore, the several occurrences of the cognate verb usually refer to a "turning away" that amounts to "apostasy," a deliberate and antagonistic rejection of Christ....Therefore, this noun, which was rendered "falling away" in the KJV, in more recent English translations has been correctly rendered "rebellion." In secular Greek, in fact, the word was used to refer to a political or military revolt, *not in the sense* of "falling

away" from a position once held, but of a rebellion against a power or deity to whom one was not committed.[9]

This is the proper nuance as found in the Greek. Another way to express the committing of apostasy is making a statement of defiance against something or someone to whom one was not committed. In this case, the Jews would be making a defiant statement against Jesus and the gospel. I will explain more about this later, but for now let me provide another example. Today, most Muslims will call Christians apostates. Yet we are not those who once held on to Islam and then "fell away"; instead we defiantly reject the truth claims of Islam. It is accurate to call us apostates in this sense.

If we understand apostasy as Gordon Fee describes it from the Greek language, then it becomes quite clear that we could identify the Jewish nation as the one who commits apostasy, which is the first event of the DOTL (2 Thess. 2:3). This brings up another interesting connection to question number 2, to which we will now turn.

2. WHAT IS THE TELLTALE SIGN THAT THE SEVEN-YEAR TRIBULATION HAS BEGUN AND IS PRESENT?

According to 2 Thessalonians 2:3, it is *the* apostasy. However, we must answer this question based on Daniel 9:27, which identifies the beginning of the seventieth week of Daniel (the DOTL) with the making or establishing of a strong covenant. We do not have all the details of this covenant, but it says, "And he will confirm a covenant *with the many* for one week" (NASB, emphasis added).

The italicized phrase appears only twice in Daniel (9:27; 11:33) and is the same in Hebrew (*rab*) and the Greek Septuagint (*polys*). The 11:33 passage refers to the people of Israel historically during the abomination of the temple by Antiochus IV. (See chapter 2.) So, the telltale sign will be an agreement or covenant being made between the Antichrist and the Jewish people.

Some people on the internet in the last few years have been saying that Daniel 9:27 was speaking in reference to the United Nations making agreements with the "many" nations of the world involving the Agenda 2030 goals. This clearly cannot be the case.

Second Thessalonians 2:3—A Jewish Apostasy or Church Apostasy?

The Hebrew is specific that it will be the Antichrist making a covenant with *the many*, which is a reference to Israel (Dan. 11:33).

Several questions arise from Daniel 9:27, such as, "What is the content and makeup of this covenant made with the Antichrist? Is it a peace covenant? Does the Antichrist provide military protection for Israel? What kind of covenant is this?"

If we read the rest of Daniel 9:27 in context, some descriptive markers immediately jump out at us. For example, the very next phrase after the word *covenant* involves a time marker ("in the middle of the week") and then immediately discusses the ceasing of sacrifices and offerings. The context of this verse involves sacrifices and offerings and a covenant.

The Hebrew word for *covenant* in 9:27 is *b'riyt*. It occurs five other times in the Book of Daniel. The first is in the beginning part of this chapter when Daniel prays, "I prayed to the LORD my God and made confession, saying, 'O Lord, the great and awesome God, who keeps covenant and steadfast love with those *who love him and keep his commandments*'" (Dan. 9:4, emphasis added). This language of Daniel comes directly from Deuteronomy 5:10 and 7:9, which recount the Mosaic covenant. The other references are all in chapter 11 (vv. 22, 28, 30, 32) and also all refer to the Mosaic covenant.

This is important to keep in mind as we seek to understand the covenant of Daniel 9:27. I find it unlikely that right in the middle of this chapter Daniel would introduce a covenant that is completely foreign to the context and the rest of the book. To try and force modern "peace agreement" language for a "covenant" on Daniel 9:27 is problematic. I am not the only one to pick up on this inconsistency.

Paul Tanner comments on Daniel 9:27 in his *Evangelical Exegetical Commentary* on the Book of Daniel. He writes:

> The problem with this view is that there is nothing in the context to support the idea that a peace treaty or covenant of protection is in view, nor is this thesis taught elsewhere in Scripture. Yet the context of Daniel 9:27 does support an alternative view. The fact that he eventually "puts an end to sacrifice and offering" suggests that this covenant has

something to do with the ancient Mosaic law. If the antichrist's purpose is to masquerade and deceive the Jewish people into thinking he is the real Messiah, then it makes sense that this covenant in Daniel 9:27 is related to the Mosaic law.[10]

In connection with the Hebrew verb of Daniel 9:27 (NASB), "He will *make* a firm covenant," Tanner highlights some helpful background information:

> The *Hipʻil* of *gāḇar* in Daniel 9:27, then, might mean something like "he will cause a covenant to be strong or great for the many." This does not seem to lend support to the idea that the covenant itself is "strong," much less that he "confirms" the covenant. Rather, the idea seems to be that he strongly establishes a covenant with the many, or perhaps that he enforces a covenant (he causes it to prevail or be binding).[11]

He continues:

> In light of the contextual clue about "sacrifice and offering," the words "make a covenant" are best understood to mean that the antichrist will pose as a false messiah who dupes Israel (at least initially) and causes the Mosaic covenant to prevail in the land (i.e., he enforces it). Actually, the expectation in orthodox Jewish eschatology is that Messiah will uphold the Mosaic law and usher in an age of righteousness.[12]

These comments are quite helpful in that they provide great understanding about the nature and substance of the covenant made between the Antichrist and Israel. The rabbinic Jews are desperate to enforce the Mosaic covenant on all the various sectors of modern Israeli society. In fact, there has been much pushback from the secular demographic in Israel against the Mosaic covenant elements, such as Sabbath restrictions for businesses and public transportation. The rabbis are not happy that the full Mosaic system is not in place in all of Israeli society. Therefore, if the time came for a strong leader to arise and make good on enforcing the Mosaic covenant across the entire land of Israel, the religious Jews would be very open to this person. Jesus reveals that in the future the Jewish leadership will receive a person just like this. Read on in question number 3.

3. Who is Jesus talking about in John 5:43? What does it mean for the Jews to receive this other person (as Messiah or Christ)?

"I have come in my Father's name, and you do not receive me. If another comes in his own name, you will receive him" (John 5:43). If we follow the flow of John's narrative, we see that Jesus admits that He is the Messiah to the woman at the well (John 4:25-26). This admission was quite rare in His public ministry and sets the stage for John's writing in chapter 5.

Jesus says another will come in his own name and the Jews will receive that person. What does it mean for the Jews to receive this other person? It shouldn't be that difficult because the fact that they didn't receive Jesus as Messiah is obvious. So, the Jewish people, who in the first century rejected Jesus as Messiah, will receive another who comes in his own name as messiah or Christ, also known as the Antichrist.

The question now before us with regard to John 5:43 is, When does this *receiving* event happen? I imagine most prophecy teachers would agree that the reception of this Antichrist will most likely happen at the time when the covenant is arranged between the Jewish people and the Antichrist (cf. Dan. 9:27).

I would contend that this event—the Jews confirming a covenant with the Antichrist—is *the apostasy* as spoken of in 2 Thessalonians 2:3, which we have already determined to be the first event of the seven-year DOTL. The timing, context, and parties involved all match up perfectly.

Most prophecy teachers consider the first seal of Revelation 6:2 to be a reference to the Antichrist. A large consensus also interpret the start of the tribulation period (the DOTL) as beginning in Revelation 6:2. The seven-year tribulation DOTL begins with the advent of the Antichrist, and we also know he is involved in the confirming of the covenant. This fits perfectly with what I see Paul saying in 2 Thessalonians 2:3. The DOTL cannot be present unless the apostasy comes first (the Jews agreeing to the covenant) and the man of lawlessness ("man of sin" in the KJV) is revealed as the one who strengthens the covenant. These two items happen simultaneously as we match up Daniel 9:27; John 5:43; Revelation 6:1-2; and 2 Thessalonians 2:3.

4. When will the Jews receive this other person as Christ?

In John 5:43 we see that the Jews receive the one coming in his own name when they receive his authority and establishment of the Mosaic covenant throughout the land of Israel (Dan. 9:27) at the beginning of the seventieth week (seven-year tribulation). The reestablishment of the Mosaic covenant in the land of Israel also must include the reinstatement of sacrifices and offerings, which would require that a temple be built in order to fulfill the commandments of the Law of Moses concerning the temple rituals. All this would presuppose that the red heifer ritual has already been accomplished so that the ashes could be mixed with water and purify the Temple Mount and the people.

5. In 2 Thessalonians 2:3 it says *the* apostasy. If this is the apostasy of the *church*, how will we know exactly when it happens?

As mentioned previously in Andy Woods' comments, the definite article causes confusion when trying to connect this to the church but poses no problem when connecting it with a Jewish apostasy. Robert Thomas does not specifically address the nature of the apostasy in his article. This makes sense, since his article focused on the teaching of imminency.

In his Thessalonians commentary in the *Expositor's Bible Commentary*, Thomas does not get specific about what the apostasy involves.[13] He suggests it could be a rebellion by those who professed Christianity but were left behind in the rapture. Based on his clear understanding of the text, he says that whatever the apostasy involves, it happens *within* the DOTL. Therefore, Thomas knows that this cannot be an apostasy of the church. The church is removed in the rapture prior to the DOTL. This apostasy happens within the DOTL and must involve some other group, which he surmises might be professing Christians who were left behind. This is plausible but doesn't fit the context of the DOTL, specifically when we see it bleed over into the discussion of the temple in verse 4, which we all would agree is very Jewish in context.

6. IF 2 THESSALONIANS 2:3 REFERS TO *THE* APOSTASY OF THE *JEWS*, HOW WILL WE KNOW EXACTLY WHEN IT HAPPENS?

It will be easy for the people present after the rapture to recognize this singular act of apostasy by the Jewish leadership as they make a covenant with the Antichrist. Charles Wanamaker, in *The Epistles to the Thessalonians: A Commentary on the Greek Text*, sees the apostasy as a Jewish rebellion. He writes:

> In the apocalyptic context of 2 Thessalonians 2, the rebellion referred to is a religious one directed against God. In all probability we may identify those whose rebellion is mentioned in v. 3 with those who are to be deceived in vv. 10-12. While Paul may have thought of certain Christians being involved (elsewhere he questioned the bona fides of some who purported to be Christians: cf. Gal. 2:4; 2 Cor. 11:12-15; Phil. 1:15-18), the reference to the temple in v. 4 suggests that he is working with a traditional apocalyptic understanding in which it was maintained that many of the people of God, *that is the Jews*, would rebel against God and the Law at the time of the end (cf. Jub. 23:14-23; 2 Esdr. 5:1-13; 1 Enoch 91:3-10; 93:8-10; 1QpHab 2:1ff. and Mk. 13:5f.).[14]

What Will the Antichrist's Message and Talking Points Be?

This is an interesting question. It is amazing that we do not have to guess what the Antichrist will say and do. We know he will speak blasphemous tirades against God (Dan. 11:36; 7:25; Rev. 13:6). Additionally, and more specifically, John tells us exactly what one of his lies will be: "Children, it is the last hour, and as you have heard that antichrist is coming, so now many antichrists have come. Therefore, we know that it is the last hour....*Who is the liar but he who denies that Jesus is the Christ* [Messiah]? This is the antichrist, he who denies the Father and the Son" (1 John 2:18, 22, emphasis added). This is an amazing passage in that it reveals that one of the main selling points of the coming Antichrist will be to deny that Jesus is the Messiah! Instead, he will take the title himself and deceive the Jews into believing he is the Messiah.

John also makes note that the Antichrist will speak specific blasphemies against Jesus. He writes, "For many deceivers have gone out into the world, those who do not confess the coming of Jesus [Messiah] in the flesh. Such a one is the deceiver and the antichrist" (2 John 1:7). We also know that when the Antichrist comes, he will speak with flattery (Dan. 11:21, 32, 34) and demonstrate his false authority by producing miraculous signs and wonders, which will help accomplish his deception (Rev. 13:13; 2 Thess. 2:9).

When the Antichrist comes on the scene, he will have the authority and position to offer the Jewish people a certain level of security and the ability to enforce the Mosaic covenant in the entire land of Israel. The rabbinic Jews will embrace this wholeheartedly. In fact, their view on eschatology is that when the Messiah comes, he will uphold the Mosaic Law in the land of Israel and will be involved in rebuilding the third temple. They will believe the Antichrist to be their Messiah. He will require them to repudiate Jesus as Messiah, which they will be glad to do. This fresh act of rebellion against Jesus and embracing this false Messiah will be a blatant act of apostasy and will kick off the seventieth week of Daniel (the DOTL).

Let's compare all the elements we have examined so far (see

Second Thessalonians 2:3—A Jewish Apostasy or Church Apostasy?

the left side of the following chart) and see what was spoken in Daniel 9:27 and 2 Thessalonians 2:3. Notice that the events and characteristics that start the tribulation period line up quite nicely in both texts.

START OF THE DAY OF THE LORD	DANIEL 9:27	2 THESSALONIANS 2:3
Singular person Antichrist	He makes a covenant for seven years	Man of lawlessness revealed
Day of the Lord FIRST event	Making of the covenant STARTS seventieth week	Apostasy is FIRST event
John 5:43—Jesus rejected as Messiah	Singular figure makes covenant with the Jewish people. Jews receive AC as Messiah?	Receiving of AC and his authority for the covenant or an apostasy?
Church is removed prior to the day of the Lord	Seventieth week begins, church cannot be around	Apostasy happens as first event inside the day of the Lord. How can this be the church?
The message of the covenant	Covenant reinstituting the Mosaic covenant and building of the Third Temple	A fresh repudiation of Jesus as NOT being the Messiah which is a SINGULAR apostasy involving the man of lawlessness
Context	Seventieth week of Daniel is exclusively Jewish (9:24)	Paul is writing to the Thessalonians about the DOTL which the church is 100 percent not involved in (i.e. Jewish)
Context	Covenant involving sacrifices and offerings ceasing	Paul immediately discusses the involvement of the Temple

Let me add one more piece of information as we wrap up this appendix. The demographics of Israel today are quite surprising. It is estimated that almost half the population is secular or atheist.[15] Most of the secular population does not care about religion, the rebuilding of the temple, or the Mosaic Law. In fact, there is much tension in Israeli society today between the religious and the secular.

When the time comes for the Antichrist to arrive on the scene and offer the Jewish people the ability to reinstate the Mosaic Law and rebuild the temple, why will the secular percent of the population even care? This is something I have pondered. We know that some event must take place which causes a change in the secular population. This event would have to be monumental to get them to become theists and turn toward God.

One future event that I believe could serve as the catalyst for this change in the secular Jewish population is the Gog and Magog war spoken of in Ezekiel 38–39. During this war, Israel will be completely alone with no one—including the US—to help her. She will be up against the wall, facing a large contingent of super-powerful armies (Russia, Iran, Turkey, and so on). When Israel is close to losing this war and facing annihilation, God will do something earth shattering from heaven.

Ezekiel writes:

> But on that day, the day that Gog shall come against the land of Israel, declares the Lord GOD, my wrath will be roused in my anger. For in my jealousy and in my blazing wrath I declare, on that day there shall be a *great earthquake* in the land of Israel. The fish of the sea and the birds of the heavens and the beasts of the field and all creeping things that creep on the ground, and all the people who are on the face of the earth, shall quake at my presence. And the mountains shall be thrown down, and the cliffs shall fall, and every wall shall tumble to the ground. I will summon a sword against Gog on all my mountains, declares the Lord GOD. Every man's sword will be against his brother. With pestilence and bloodshed I will enter into judgment with him, and I will rain upon him and his hordes and the many peoples who are with him *torrential rains and hailstones, fire and*

sulfur. So I will show my greatness and my holiness and make myself known in the eyes of many nations. Then they will know that I am the LORD.
—EZEKIEL 38:18–23, EMPHASIS ADDED

God will supernaturally intervene in this war in a way that is undeniable by the world and Israel. All of Israel's enemies will be supernaturally destroyed in a short time. We do not know the exact timing of this event. Imagine in this scenario that the rapture has just taken place and immediately after this, God leads His hordes in an attack on Israel and saves her in a dramatic way.

Notice also what God says in the following chapter. Ezekiel writes, "And I will set my glory among the nations, and all the nations shall see my judgment that I have executed, and my hand that I have laid on them. The *house of Israel shall know that I am the LORD their God, from that day forward*" (Ezek. 39:21–22, emphasis added). Some people assume that because Israel comes to know that the Lord is their God, this equals salvation. This doesn't have to be the case. What it could do is turn the secular population into theists, and they will then turn to the rabbis for spiritual guidance. The rabbis will embrace this newfound attention and seek to guide them in following Moses, which is all they know.

Imagine also at this exact time the Antichrist (false Messiah) shows up on the scene and performs miracles and begins to speak for God while promising Jews the freedom to reinstitute the Mosaic Law throughout the land of Israel and rebuild their temple. All they have to do is deny that Jesus is Messiah and put their trust in him. *Apostasy* occurs, and this begins the DOTL and the seventieth week of Daniel. No one knows exactly how things will play out, but this conjectural narrative is quite plausible.

IN CONCLUSION

It is important to say that we are no doubt currently living in the age of the Laodicean church (Rev. 3:14–22), which has become apostate. We also know that 1 Timothy 4:1 says, "Now the Spirit expressly says that in later times some will depart from the faith by devoting themselves to deceitful spirits and teachings of demons."

This is undeniable, but we know that it did not happen in a singular specified event as 2 Thessalonians 2:3 requires; it began in the mid-1800s when seminaries and Christian universities began to embrace theologically liberal doctrines. We have watched as it has become more pervasive over the last century, and now most of the mainline denominations no longer emphasize the main tenets of the gospel.

If we take this understanding of *the* apostasy into consideration, we will not be looking for some specific, singular, instantaneous apostasy of the church but rather recognizing that *the* apostasy refers to the Jewish reception of the Antichrist and their entering into a covenant with him.

Christians in England, Canada, and the United States are entering into a time of increased hostility, censorship, harassment, ostracization, arrests, and potential physical persecution. Just like with the Thessalonians, none of this should convince us that we are in the tribulation period (DOTL). We know that the DOTL cannot be present because the Jewish apostasy and the revealing of the Antichrist have not occurred. Praise the Lord that we have the promise of being rescued prior to the arrival of the DOTL (Luke 17:22-37; 21:34-36; Rev. 3:10). In the meantime, we are to remain watching (Mark 13:37) and to be busy about the kingdom business (Luke 19:13), appreciating that God is allowing more time for people to come to repentance (2 Pet. 3:9). Amen and amen!

For more information and to watch my presentations on this subject, please visit prophecywatchers.com/apostasy.

Appendix B

ALFRED EDERSHEIM ON THE TEMPLE'S MINISTRY AND SERVICES AT THE TIME OF CHRIST

ALFRED EDERSHEIM (1825–1889) was a Messianic Jewish believer who studied the rabbinical writings along with the Old Testament. He wrote extensively on the New Testament from a Jewish perspective. I recommend his writings as a good foundation to understand the Jewish frame of reference.

The following is an excerpt from his book *The Temple, Its Ministry and Services as They Were at the Time of Jesus Christ*.

SIGNIFICANCE OF THE RED HEIFER

This is not the place more fully to vindicate the views here propounded. Without some deeper symbolical meaning attaching to them, the peculiarities of the sin-offering of the red heifer would indeed be well-nigh unintelligible. This must be substantially the purport of a Jewish tradition to the effect that King Solomon, who knew the meaning of all God's ordinances, was unable to understand that of the red heifer. A "Haggadah" maintains that the wisest of men had in Ecclesiastes 7:23 thus described his experience in this respect: "All this have I proved by wisdom," that is, all other matters; "I said, I will be wise," that is, in reference to the meaning of the red heifer; "but it was far from me." But if Jewish traditionalism was thus conscious of its spiritual ignorance in regard to this type, it was none the less zealous in prescribing, with even more than usual precision, its ceremonial. The first object was to obtain a proper "red heifer" for the sacrifice. The *Mishnah* states the needful age of such a *red heifer* as from two to four, and even five years; the color of its hide, two white or black hairs springing from the *same follicle* disqualifying it; and how, if she have been put to any use, though only a cloth had been laid on her, she would no longer answer the requirement that upon her "never came yoke."

THE SACRIFICE OF THE RED HEIFER

Even more particular are the Rabbis to secure that the sacrifice be properly offered. Seven days before, the priest destined for the service was separated and kept in the Temple—in "the House of Stoves"—where he was daily sprinkled with the ashes—as the Rabbis fable—of all the red heifers ever offered. When bringing the sacrifice, he was to wear his white priestly raiments. According to their tradition, there was an arched roadway leading from the east gate of the Temple out upon the Mount of Olives—double arched, that is, arched also over the supporting pillars, for fear of any possible pollution through the ground upwards. Over this the procession passed. On the Mount of Olives the elders of Israel were already in waiting. First, the priest immersed his whole body, then he approached the pile of cedar-, pine-, and fig-wood which was heaped like a pyramid, but having an opening in the middle, looking towards the west. Into this the red heifer was thrust, and bound, with its head towards the south and its face looking to the west, the priest standing east of the sacrifice, his face, of course, also turned westwards. Slaying the sacrifice with his right hand, he caught up the blood in his left. Seven times he dipped his finger in it, sprinkling it towards the Most Holy Place, which he was supposed to have in full view over the Porch of Solomon or through the eastern gate. Then, immediately descending, he kindled the fire. As soon as the flames burst forth, the priest, standing outside the pit in which the pile was built up, took cedarwood, hyssop, and "scarlet" wool, asking three times as he held up each: "Is this cedarwood? Is this hyssop? Is this scarlet?" so as to call to the memory of every one the Divine ordinance. Then tying them together with the scarlet wool, he threw the bundle upon the burning heifer. The burnt remains were beaten into ashes by sticks or stone mallets and passed through coarse sieves; then divided into three parts—one of which was kept in the Temple-terrace (the *Chel*), the other on the Mount of Olives, and the third distributed among the priesthood throughout the land.

CHILDREN USED IN THE OFFERING

The next care was to find one to whom no suspicion of possible defilement could attach, who might administer purification to such as needed it. For this purpose a priest was not required; but any one—even a child—was fit for the service. In point of fact, according to Jewish tradition, children were exclusively employed in this ministry. If we are to believe the *Mishnah*, there were at Jerusalem certain dwellings built upon rocks, that were hollowed beneath, so as to render impossible pollution from unknown graves beneath. Here the children destined for this ministry were to be born, and here they were reared and kept till fit for their service. Peculiar precautions were adopted in leading them out to their work. The child was to ride on a bullock, and to mount and descend it by boards. He was first to proceed to the Pool of *Siloam* [or the *Gihon* spring], and to fill a stone cup with its water, and thence to ride to the Temple Mount, which, with all its courts, was also supposed to be free from possible pollutions by being hollowed beneath.

Dismounting, he would approach the "Beautiful Gate," where the vessel with the ashes of the red heifer was kept. Next a goat would be brought out, and a rope, with a stick attached to it, tied between its horns. The stick was put into the vessel with the ashes, the goat driven backwards, and of the ashes thereby spilt the child would take for use in the sacred service so much as to be visible upon the water. It is only fair to add, that one of the Mishnic sages, deprecating a statement which might be turned into ridicule by the Sadducees, declares that any clean person might take with his hand from the vessel so much of the ashes as was required for the service. The purification was made by sprinkling with hyssop. According to the Rabbis, three separate stalks, each with a blossom on it, were tied together, and the tip of these blossoms dipped into the water of separation, the hyssop itself being grasped while sprinkling the unclean. The same authorities make the most incredible assertion that altogether, from the time of Moses to the final destruction of the Temple, only seven, or else nine, such red heifers had been offered: the first by Moses, the second by Ezra, and the other five, or else seven, between the time of Ezra and that of the taking of Jerusalem by the Romans. We only add that the cost of this sacrifice, which was always great, since a pure red heifer was very rare, was defrayed from the Temple treasury, as being offered for the whole people. Those who lived in the country would, for purification from defilement by the dead, come up to Jerusalem seven days before the great festivals, and, as part of the ashes were distributed among the priesthood, there could never be any difficulty in purifying houses or vessels.[1]

Appendix C

JOSEPHUS DISCUSSES THE RED HEIFER

JOSEPHUS WAS A first-century Jewish historian who participated in the great revolt against Rome in AD 66–70. While serving as a Jewish general in Galilee, he was captured and became a historian, primarily for Rome. He wrote the following about the red heifer:

> **6.** (78) Then it was that Miriam, the sister of Moses, came to her end, having completed her fortieth year since she left Egypt, on the first day of the lunar month Xanthicus. They then made a public funeral for her, at a great expense. She was buried upon a certain mountain, which they call Sin; and when they had mourned for her thirty days, Moses purified the people after this manner: (79) He brought a heifer that had never been used to the plough or to husbandry, that was complete in all its parts, and entirely of a red color, at a little distance from the camp, into a place perfectly clean. This heifer was slain by the high priest, and her blood sprinkled with his finger seven times before the tabernacle of God; (80) after this, the entire heifer was burnt in that state, together with its skin and entrails; and they threw cedar wood, and hyssop, and scarlet wool, into the midst of the fire; then a clean man gathered all her ashes together, and laid them in a place perfectly clean. (81) When therefore any persons were defiled by a dead body, they put a little of these ashes into spring water, with hyssop, and, dipping part of these ashes in it, they sprinkled them with it, both on the third day, and on the seventh, and after that they were clean. This he enjoined them to do also when the tribes should come into their own land.[1]

Notes

CHAPTER 1
1. Barry Holtz, "The Mystery of the Red Heifer," The Jewish Theological Seminary, June 19, 2010, https://www.jtsa.edu/torah/the-mystery-of-the-red-heifer/.
2. Moses ben Maimon, *The Guide for the Perplexed* Part 3 26, Sefaria.org, accessed November 13, 2024, https://www.sefaria.org/Guide_for_the_Perplexed%2C_Part_3.26.1?lang=bi&with=all&lang2=en.

CHAPTER 2
1. "The 'Al-Aksa Is in Danger' Libel: The History of a Lie—2. Israel Relinquishes the Temple Mount," Jerusalem Center for Security and Foreign Affairs, accessed November 20, 2024, https://jcpa.org/al-aksa-is-in-danger-libel/al-aksa-is-in-danger-libel-temple-mount/.
2. You can find my article and presentation at prophecywatchers.com/watching-israel.
3. Josephus, *Antiquities of the Jews, Book XII*, ch. 5.4, accessed November 13, 2024, https://ccel.org/j/josephus/works/ant-12.htm.
4. To read more about the seven-year tribulation period known as the "day of the Lord," see https://www.raptureready.com/2022/02/10/does-wrath-of-god-begin-after-6th-seal-is-opened-by-mondo-gonzales/.
5. Jeffrey A. D. Weima, *Baker Exegetical Commentary on the New Testament: 1-2 Thessalonians*, ed. Robert W. Yarbrough and Robert H. Stein (Baker Academic, 2014), 522.
6. *Hippolytus of Rome: Treatise on Christ and Antichrist*, paragraph 6, Early Christian Writings, accessed November 13, 2024, https://www.earlychristianwritings.com/text/hippolytus-christ.html.
7. Cyril of Jerusalem, *Catechetical Lectures*, 15.15, https://www.newadvent.org/fathers/310115.htm.
8. William E. Blackstone, *Jesus Is Coming* (Fleming H. Revell, 1898), 108–109, https://archive.org/details/JesusIsComing-raptureByWilliamW.e.b.Blackstone.

CHAPTER 4
1. Gordon J. Wenham, *Tyndale Old Testament Commentaries: Numbers* (Intervarsity Press Academic, 2008), 163.
2. Jacob Milgrom, *The JPS Torah Commentary: Numbers* (Jewish Publication Society, 1990), 158.
3. Milgrom, *The JPS Torah Commentary*, 158.

4. Milgrom, *The JPS Torah Commentary*, 160.
5. Milgrom, *The JPS Torah Commentary*, 161.
6. Milgrom, *The JPS Torah Commentary*, 162.

CHAPTER 5

1. *The Lexham Bible Dictionary*, s.v. "Rabbinic Literature and the New Testament," accessed November 19, 2024, https://app.logos.com/books/LLS%3ALBD/headwords/Rabbinic%20Literature%20and%20the%20New%20Testament?headwordLanguage=en.
2. "Mishnah," Jewish Virtual Library, accessed November 13, 2024, https://www.jewishvirtuallibrary.org/mishnah.
3. Sefaria.org, s.v. "Kiddushin 4:12," accessed November 13, 2024, https://www.sefaria.org/Mishnah_Kiddushin.4.12?lang=bi.
4. Sefaria.org, s.v. "Kiddushin 4:14," accessed November 13, 2024, https://www.sefaria.org/Mishnah_Kiddushin.4.14?lang=bi.
5. Jacob Neusner, *The Mishnah: A New Translation* (Yale University Press, 1988), 1012–1013.
6. Rabbi Chaim Richman, *The Mystery of the Red Heifer: Divine Promise of Purity* (Richman, 1977), 21.
7. "Targum Jonathan on Numbers 19," trans. John Wesley Etheridge, 1862, Sefaria.org, accessed November 20, 2024, https://www.sefaria.org/Targum_Jonathan_on_Numbers.19.2?lang=bi.
8. Neusner, *The Mishnah*, 1015; brackets in original.
9. Jacob Neusner, *The Babylonian Talmud: A Translation and Commentary*, vol. 21a (Hendrickson Publishers, 2011), 114.
10. "The Divine Ordinance of Purification Through the Ashes of the RED HEIFER, as Outlined in the Book of Numbers, Chapter 19," Temple Institute, accessed November 19, 2024, https://templeinstitute.org/red-heifer-numbers-19/.
11. Rabbi Moshe ben Maimon ("Maimonides"); translated by Eliyahu Touger, "Parah Adumah—Chapter 1," Chabad.org, accessed November 19, 2024, https://www.chabad.org/library/article_cdo/aid/1517254/jewish/Parah-Adumah-Chapter-1.htm.
12. Neusner, *The Mishnah*, 1016.
13. Rabbi Moshe ben Maimon ("Maimonides"); translated by Eliyahu Touger, "Parah Adumah—Chapter 3," Chabad.org, accessed November 19, 2024, https://www.chabad.org/library/article_cdo/aid/1517256/jewish/Parah-Adumah-Chapter-3.htm, emphasis added.
14. "About Us: Who Is Boneh Israel?," Boneh Israel, accessed November 19, 2024, https://www.bonehisrael.com.
15. "Bible Prophecy Update: Red Heifers," Prophecy Watchers, accessed November 26, 2024, https://www.youtube.com/watch?v=uisrUTS7jyg.
16. Map by Daniel M. Wright, createdwright.com. Used with permission.

17. Joseph Good, "Chavurah—The Red Heifer: Addressing Details and Questions," Facebook, September 28, 2022, https://www.facebook.com/joseph.good.18/videos/1923392387866289/.
18. Arnold G. Fruchtenbaum, *The Footsteps of the Messiah* (Ariel Ministries, 2020).
19. Neusner, *The Mishnah*, 1014. Brackets in original.
20. Ben Maimon, "Parah Adumah—Chapter 1," emphasis added.
21. Jacob Neusner, *The Jerusalem Talmud: A Translation and Commentary* (Hendrickson Publishers, 2008), emphasis added.
22. For a full source list for this story and to explore how it appears in various writings visit https://www.encyclopedia.com/religion/encyclopedias-almanacs-transcripts-and-maps/dama-son-netina.
23. Neusner, *The Mishnah*, 1016. Brackets in original.
24. Ben Maimon, "Parah Adumah—Chapter 3," emphasis added.

CHAPTER 6

1. Nate Orbach, "The Temple Mount Movement Braces for Its Moment, *+972 Magazine*, March 20, 2023, https://www.972mag.com/temple-mount-movement-jerusalem.
2. Judah Ari Gross, "Fighting Rabbinic Ban, Jewish Activists Push Temple Mount Prayer Toward Mainstream," *Times of Israel*, June 2, 2022, https://www.timesofisrael.com/fighting-rabbinic-ban-jewish-activists-bring-temple-mount-worship-out-of-fringes/.
3. Jewish News Service Update Desk, "Record Number of Jews Visit the Temple Mount," *Jewish News Service*, September 11, 2024, https://www.jns.org/record-number-of-jews-visit-the-temple-mount/.
4. Chen Shalita, "Torah First: The Judicial Revolution No One Is Talking About," Shomrim, January 12, 2023, https://www.shomrim.news/eng/torah-first-the-judicial-revolution-no-one-is-talking-about.
5. Jeremy Sharon, "Fire on the Mount? How the New Government Might Shift Policy at Flashpoint Holy Site," *Times of Israel*, November 6, 2022, https://www.timesofisrael.com/fire-on-the-mount-how-the-new-government-might-shift-policy-at-flashpoint-holy-site/.
6. "Israel Committed to Temple Mount Status Quo, Herzog Tells US Envoy," *Jewish National Syndicate*, September 8, 2024, https://www.jns.org/israel-committed-to-temple-mount-status-quo-herzog-tells-us-envoy/.
7. Charles Bybelezer, "Ben-Gvir: Jews Can Pray at Temple Mount; PM: No Change in Status Quo," *Jewish National Syndicate*, August 26, 2024, https://www.jns.org/ben-gvir-jews-can-pray-at-temple-mount-pm-no-change-in-status-quo/.
8. Jacob Magid, "Galilee 'Loaves' Church Arsonist Sentenced to Four Years," *Times of Israel*, December 12, 2017, https://www.timesofisrael.com/galilee-loaves-church-arsonist-sentenced-to-4-years/.

9. Joel C. Rosenberg, "Israeli Interior Ministry Apologizes to Christian Zionist Groups, Will Resume Issuing Clergy Visas for Their Staffs," All Israel News, September 14, 2023, https://allisrael.com/israeli-interior-ministry-apologizes-to-christian-zionist-groups-will-resume-issuing-clergy-visas-for-their-staffs.
10. "Ben Gvir Ascends Temple Mount in Jerusalem on Tisha B'Av, Causing Arab Uproar," All Israel News, July 27, 2023, https://allisrael.com/ben-gvir-ascends-temple-mount-in-jerusalem-on-tisha-b-av-causing-arab-uproar.
11. You can read more about Robert Mawire at israelallies.org/dr-robert-mawire.

CHAPTER 7

1. Richard Gottheil and Samuel Krauss, "Bar Kokba and Bar Kokba War," Jewish Encyclopedia.com, accessed November 20, 2024, https://jewishencyclopedia.com/articles/2471-bar-kokba-and-bar-kokba-war#anchor3. This entry also provides ancient sources for reference.
2. Richard Gottheil and Michael Adler, "Julian the Apostate (Flavius Claudius Julianus)," Jewish Encyclopedia.com, accessed November 20, 2024, https://jewishencyclopedia.com/articles/9078-julian-the-apostate-flavius-claudius-julianus.
3. Wikipedia, s.v. "Third Temple," accessed November 20, 2024, https://en.wikipedia.org/wiki/Third_Temple.
4. See also "Sacred Vessels and Vestments of the Holy Temple," Temple Institute, accessed November 15, 2024, https://templeinstitute.org/gallery/.
5. The Temple Institute, "Holy Temple Building Plans Playlist," YouTube, accessed November 20, 2024, https://www.youtube.com/playlist?app=desktop&list=PLPtr_UmiMgfy5WzkyI3Nl1r88SPrJE2RU.
6. Yaakov Levi, "Temple Institute Raises $100K for 3rd Temple Plan," Israel National News, September 28, 2014, https://www.israelnationalnews.com/news/185556.
7. Adam Eliyahu Berkowitz, "Jews Begin Building Third Temple on Israel Independence Day," Israel365News, May 6, 2022, https://israel365news.com/352915/jews-begin-building-third-temple-on-israel-independence-day/.
8. Adam Eliyahu Berkowitz, "Creating Handmade Wooden Flutes for the Third Temple," Israel365News, December 26, 2022, https://israel365news.com/364303/creating-handmade-wooden-flutes-for-the-third-temple/.
9. Adam Eliyahu Berkowitz, "What Is the Last Secret to be Revealed Before the Messiah?," Israel365News, May 31, 2016, https://israel365news.com/307703/watch-music-of-king-davids-time-to-be-recreated-for-third-temple-05-16/.

10. Rivkah Lambert Adler, "When the Third Temple Is Built, These Temple Priests Will Be Ready To Serve," Israel365News, October 30, 2020, https://israel365news.com/341563/when-the-third-temple-is-built-these-temple-priests-will-be-ready-to-serve/.
11. Chris Livesay, "What These Red Cows from Texas Have to Do with War and Peace in the Middle East," CBS News, March 5, 2024, https://www.cbsnews.com/news/israel-war-hamas-red-heifers-from-texas-jerusalem-jewish-temple-al-aqsa/.
12. Several sources have shared this information with me confidentially, but the details are not being made public.
13. Chris Mitchell, "Prophetic Anticipation Builds: Unblemished Red Heifers for Temple Ceremony Soon Come of Age," CBN News, March 17, 2023, https://cbn.com/news/israel/prophetic-anticipation-builds-unblemished-red-heifers-temple-ceremony-soon-come-age.
14. Adam Eliyahu Berkowitz, "Exclusive: Burning of Heifer Takes Place in Preparation for Third Temple," Israel365News, August 15, 2019, https://israel365news.com/332690/exclusive-burning-red-heifer-takes-place-preparation-third-temple/.
15. Berkowitz, "Exclusive: Burning of Heifer Takes Place in Preparation for Third Temple."
16. Berkowitz, "Exclusive: Burning of Heifer Takes Place in Preparation for Third Temple."
17. Berkowitz, "Exclusive: Burning of Heifer Takes Place in Preparation for Third Temple."

CHAPTER 8

1. Erin A. Smith, "*The Late Great Planet Earth* Made the Apocalypse a Popular Concern," *Humanities* 38, no. 1 (2017), https://www.neh.gov/humanities/2017/winter/feature/the-late-great-planet-earth-made-the-apocalypse-popular-concern.
2. Richman, *The Mystery of the Red Heifer.*
3. Richman, *The Mystery of the Red Heifer.*
4. Jeff Van Hatten, "Red Heifer Update 2022," Rapture Ready, November 1, 2022, https://www.raptureready.com/2022/11/01/red-heifer-update-2022-by-jeff-van-hatten/.
5. Prophecy Watchers, "Bible Prophecy Update: Red Heifers," YouTube video, August 4, 2023, 29:38, https://www.youtube.com/watch?v=uisrUTS7jyg.
6. Tzvi Joffre, "From Texas to Israel: Red Heifers Needed for Temple Arrive," Jerusalem Post, updated April 8, 2024, https://www.jpost.com/judaism/article-717650.
7. Kassy Akiva, "The Truth About the Red Cows in Israel," *Daily Wire*, August 8, 2024, https://www.dailywire.com/news/the-truth-about-the-red-cows-in-israel.
8. Akiva, "The Truth About the Red Cows in Israel."

9. Akiva, "The Truth About the Red Cows in Israel."
10. *Daily Wire*, "Why Texan Red Heifers Were Brought to Israel—And Why It Makes Hamas So Mad," YouTube video, August 8, 2024, 5:57, https://www.youtube.com/watch?v=Kt_uuF-jzlM.
11. Akiva, "The Truth About the Red Cows in Israel."
12. Akiva, "The Truth About the Red Cows in Israel."
13. *Jerusalem Post* Staff, "Probe Reveals 6,000 Gazans Infiltrated Israel During October 7 Massacre—Report," *Jerusalem Post*, August 31, 2024, https://www.jpost.com/israel-hamas-war/article-817176; Emanuel Fabian, "Army Hits Gaza Depot Storing Oct. 7 Paragliders; Intercepts Aerial Targets Near Eilat," *Times of Jerusalem*, July 13, 2024, https://www.timesofisrael.com/army-hits-gaza-depot-storing-oct-7-paragliders-intercepts-aerial-targets-near-eilat/.
14. "What Is Hamas and Why Is It Fighting with Israel in Gaza?," BBC, October 21, 2024, https://www.bbc.com/news/world-middle-east-67039975; Anna Schecter, "UN Finds 'Clear and Convincing' Information That Hostages Have Been Raped in Gaza," NBC News, March 5, 2024, https://www.nbcnews.com/investigations/un-finds-clear-convincing-information-hostages-raped-gaza-rcna141789.
15. "What Is Hamas and Why Is It Fighting with Israel in Gaza?," BBC; Laurie Kellman, "About 30 Children Were Taken Hostage by Hamas Militants. Their Families Wait in Agony," Associated Press, updated October 27, 2023, https://apnews.com/article/children-hostages-israel-palestinians-gaza-orphan-c8e9f6dd703a9c14161eeb6ca9e25417.
16. Adam Eliyahu Berkowitz, "Hamas Spokesman: Oct 7 Attack Launched to Stop the Red Heifers," Israel365News, January 17, 2024, https://israel365news.com/382489/hamas-spokesman-oct-7-attack-launched-to-stop-the-red-heifers/. Emphasis added.
17. David Israel, "Hamas Spokesman Abu Ubaydah Reveals: We Attacked After the Jews Imported Red Heifers," *Jewish Press*, January 26, 2024, https://www.jewishpress.com/news/israel/temple-mount-har-habayit/hamas-spokesman-abu-ubaydah-reveals-we-attacked-after-the-jews-imported-red-heifers/2024/01/26/.
18. David Martin, Ed O'Keefe, and Kathryn Watson, "Biden Says US Won't Supply Israel with Weapons for Rafah Offensive," CBS News, updated May 9, 2024, https://www.cbsnews.com/news/israel-weapons-white-house-shipments/.

CHAPTER 9

1. You can find a short paper I wrote on this subject at prophecywatchers.com/salvation-in-the-old-testament/.

CHAPTER 10

1. The Temple Institute, "More About Our 5 Red Heifer Candidates," Facebook, September 19, 2022, https://www.facebook.com/templeinstitute/posts/more-about-our-5-red-heifer-candidatesas-reported-live-last-week-five-perfectly-/10151739696054969/.
2. Amir Tsarfati, "Allow me to be very honest with you...," Telegram, September 17, 2022 at 07:42, https://t.me/beholdisraelchannel/11248; Behold Israel with Amir Tsarfati, "Amir Tsarfati: The True Meaning of Rosh Hashanah," YouTube video, September 22, 2022, 21:13, https://www.youtube.com/watch?v=55lofyD8Zd4.

CHAPTER 11

1. Tuvia Pollack, "Why Do Israelis Call Jesus 'Yeshu'?" Kehila News, November 23, 2021, https://news.kehila.org/why-do-israelis-call-jesus-yeshu/.
2. Jacob Neusner, *The Babylonian Talmud: A Translation and Commentary*, vol. 5a (Hendrickson Publishers, 2011), 142. Emphasis added.

CHAPTER 12

1. Akiva, "The Truth About the Red Cows in Israel."
2. Akiva, "The Truth About the Red Cows in Israel."
3. "The Red Heifer," Temple Institute, accessed November 20, 2024, https://templeinstitute.org/para-aduma-the-red-heifer/, emphasis added.
4. Livesay, "What These Red Cows from Texas Have to Do with War and Peace in the Middle East"; "Red Cows Factor Into Israel-Hamas War," *CBS Saturday Morning*, March 2, 2024, https://www.cbs.com/shows/video/HZelbd2s_H_6pvrzgbZckLhotqZu5LQJ/.
5. CBS, "Red Cows Factor Into Israel-Hamas War."
6. @YinonMagal, "Towards Tish B'Av: Temple worshipers are now...," X, August 6, 2024, https://x.com/YinonMagal/status/1820853937786028386?ref_src=twsrc%5Etfw%7Ctwcamp%5Etweetembed%7Ctwterm%5E1820853937786028386%7Ctwgr%5E11c20b961d6512ad64ad054f599d01a97ad7b8c1%7Ctwcon%5Es1_&ref.
7. Aaron Lipkin, "Ancient Shiloh," Facebook, accessed November 26, 2024, https://www.facebook.com/aaron.lipkin.7/videos/2034858166929698.
8. Daniel B. Wallace, *Greek Grammar Beyond the Basics* (Zondervan, 1996), 729.

APPENDIX A

1. Robert Thomas, "The Rapture and the Biblical Teaching of Imminence," in *Evidence for the Rapture: A Biblical Case for Pretribulationism*, ed. John F. Hart (Moody, 2015); italics and brackets added.
2. Andy Woods, *The Falling Away: Spiritual Departure or Physical Rapture? A Second Look at 2 Thessalonians 2:3* (Dispensational Publishing House, 2018).

3. Woods, *The Falling Away*, 15.
4. Woods, *The Falling Away*, 15.
5. Woods, *The Falling Away*, 16.
6. Lee W. Brainard, *Apostasia in 2 Thessalonians 2:3: Rapture or Apostasy?* (Lee W. Brainard, 2021).
7. One of the items mentioned in Daniel 9:24 is "put an end to sin." We know this isn't the end of sin fully because there is still sin in the Millennium; therefore, the interpretation is that sin as a dominating influence is removed.
8. *American Heritage Dictionary*, s.v. "apostasy," https://www.ahdictionary.com/word/search.html?q=apostasy; GNU Collaborative International Dictionary of English, s.v. "apostasy," https://gcide.gnu.org.ua/?q=apostasy&define=Define&strategy=
9. Gordon Fee, *New International Commentary on the New Testament: The First and Second Letters to the Thessalonians* (Eerdmans, 2009), 281; emphasis added.
10. J. Paul Tanner, *Daniel: Evangelical Exegetical Commentary* (Lexham Press, 2021), 592.
11. Tanner, *Daniel*, 593.
12. Tanner, *Daniel*, 593.
13. Robert L. Thomas, Ralph Earle, and D. Edmond Hiebert, *Expositor's Bible Commentary: 1 & 2 Thessalonians, 1 & 2 Timothy, Titus* (Zondervan, 1996).
14. Charles A. Wanamaker, *The Epistles to the Thessalonians: A Commentary on the Greek Text (New International Greek Testament Commentary)* (Paternoster Press, 1990), 243–245; emphasis added.
15. Ilan Ben Zion, "Religion Has Outsized Role in Israel, Yet Most of Its Jews Aren't Really Observant," *Times of Israel*, October 5, 2023, https://www.timesofisrael.com/religion-has-outsized-role-in-israel-yet-most-of-its-jews-arent-really-observant/.

APPENDIX B

1. Alfred Edersheim, *The Temple, Its Ministry and Services as They Were at the Time of Jesus Christ* (James Clarke & Co., 1959), 351–355. Public domain.

APPENDIX C

1. Flavius Josephus *The Works of Josephus: Complete and Unabridged*, trans. William Whiston (Hendrickson, 1987), 107.

About the Author

Mondo Gonzales has been studying and teaching Bible prophecy as a pastor for more than twenty-five years. He has a bachelor's degree in biblical studies, with a concentration in Jewish studies, along with a graduate degree in biblical archaeology, giving him the necessary expertise to explain the mystery of the red heifer ritual. Gonzales is the cohost of the *Prophecy Watchers* television program, podcast, and radio program. He also directs the Psalm 19 Project. You can find him at prophecywatchers.com and being interviewed on a variety of podcasts and internet and radio shows.

Made in the USA
Monee, IL
28 April 2026